Apple
MacBook
SENIORS GUIDE

AWARD WINNING GUIDE

Empowering Seniors to Master Their MacBooks with Confidence and Ease

EASILY MASTER YOUR:
✓ **INTERNET CONNECTION**
✓ **SETTINGS**
✓ **WEB SURFING**
✓ **SOCIAL MEDIA**
✓ **EMAIL**
✓ **SECURITY**
...AND MUCH MORE!

Includes Illustrated Tips and Tricks!

BRAD JORDAN

TABLE OF CONTENTS

Free Bonus
Page 162

INTRODUCTION

PowerBook 100

Just as there are changes in life—from the way people live, travel, even eating patterns—there is also an evolution of computers. Apple laptops made their entrance in 1991 *(Moreau, 2019)*.

As the years progressed, there have been a variety of models and naming conventions. **The first machine from Apple was called PowerBook 100.** It had a trackball, set-back keyboard, and an integrated palm rest. Then came the PowerBook 500 and the PowerBook G3 in 1994. Each of the new versions released had notable improvements. In 1999, Apple released the iBook G3, prior to introducing the PowerBook Titanium G4 at the beginning of 2001. From 2006 forward, Apple introduced the MacBooks Pro and Air, with several updates achieved since then.

The Apple MacBook laptop is one of the most significant of Steve Jobs' designs. **In January 2006, the MacBook line of laptops made its first appearance** *(Ackerman, 2011; Moreau, 2019)*.

During that time, laptops were not as common as they are today, and most people who had access to computers mostly used desktops. From this time onwards, laptop prices shifted.

The price drop was dependent on the small sizes, low cost, and low-power systems that were being used in the production of laptops.

MacBook 2006

Manufacturers adopted the practice of using cheap materials to make laptops so that prices would be affordable to price-sensitive consumers. However, Apple did the opposite, they raised their standards by producing a better laptop that fetched a higher price on the market. The raised standard was a result of the groundbreaking M1 chip, which was particularly designed for the Mac laptops.

The **M1 chip** has high performance per watt, thereby allowing its users access to quicker machine learning capacities. In addition to that, the battery life of    Mac laptops and computers is double than before. Users also get access to a huge assortment of applications, as well as other outstanding features.

MacBook laptops also introduced the aspect of 'touch' for easier control and navigation. The introduction of the touch system led to the mouse phasing out. This has influenced other players to follow suit, but the MacBooks are way ahead. In the past half-decade, it turns out that the MacBook has been most influential when it comes to laptops. Not only does its price remain high but there are also other aspects as well, which makes it unique.

For instance, compared to other laptops such HDMI and SD card readers, it does not have common parts *(Ackerman, 2011)*. Apple has also shifted to making laptops that have non removable batteries.

MacBook Air - MacBook Pro - MacBook Mini

CHAPTER 1: TERMINOLOGY

Terminology Mostly Used in the Computer World

This chapter is aimed at explaining the meanings of various terms that are used in the computer world. Included in this chapter are explanations on the tangible and intangible components of the laptop. Some of the terms may be common to many technology companies, while some are specific to Apple. Let's get more details with regard to this amazing gadget.

Screenshot

A screenshot is a motionless image of whatever is shown on the screen at any given moment. It can be used to capture and show off glitches to tech-savvy friends. Screenshots may also come in handy in illustrations of tech tutorials, games, and applications, as well as photogenic moments in games. When you are using a Mac, you can take a screenshot by pressing **Shift, Command, and 4** over the area that you want to capture.

There are various other techniques when you want to capture the entire screen or an individual window. For example, go to the application menu and select File. Afterward, click on **Take Screenshot**. Select which part of the screen you want to capture, then choose **Take a Screenshot**. You could also press **Shift, Command, and 5** on your keyboard.

Screenshot - Shift > Command > 5

Software

The term 'software' refers to a set of instructions that tells a computer or laptop how to perform a particular task. The main types of software include **application and systems software**. Application software is one that is added to the computer system to enable the user to do a certain task.

For instance, a browser allows you to view pages on the internet, and a word processor enables you to type a document. Other examples of application software include spreadsheets, database management, email programs, media players, translation, and desktop publishing.

The **system software** assists with the management and running of a computer or laptop. The system software acts as the interface between application software, hardware, and the user. Among the many functions of the system software are managing storage space, allocating system resources, providing security, and retrieving files The main types of systems software that you should know include device drivers, operating system, utility, and programming software *(Wang, n.d)*.

The **operating system** coordinates and controls the computer's hardware, software, and applications. Without the operating system, a laptop or computer will not be able to function. The operating system boots the computer, handles input and output, and manages files and resources. Examples of operating systems include Apple iOS, macOS, Linux, and Android OS.

Utility software is one that assists in setting up, configuring, analyzing, strengthening. and maintaining a computer. Utility softwares perform specific functions. It functions as a backup software, screen saver, memory tester, and an antivirus.

Another type of system software of importance is the **device driver**, which controls a specific hardware that is connected to the computer. A device driver's main function is to act as a translator between the hardware and operating systems, or other applications that utilize it. It gives commands to the computer on how to communicate with the device by translating the operating system's set of instructions into a language that is understandable to the device. At the end of the day, the device can perform the required task. Examples of device drivers include **USB, motherboard, display, and sound card drivers.**

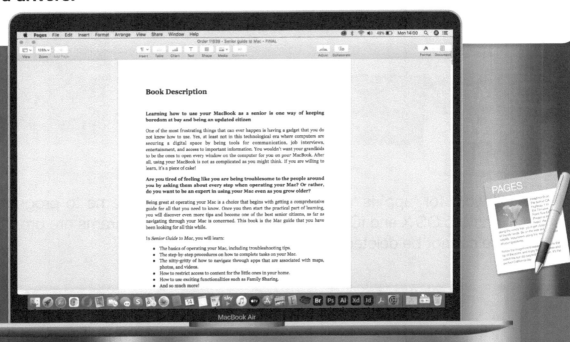

Hardware

The physical components of a computer are referred to as hardware. Hardware is further divided into two categories, which are the internal and external hardware. External hardware devices are those that are located outside the computer. The external hardware is further classified into input and output devices. An input device can enhances the process of entering information into a computer or laptop so that it can be processed.

Output devices receive information from the computer to produce the desired result. **Examples of external hardware include the mouse, keyboard, touchpad, microphone, webcam, speaker, screen, and headphones**. Internal hardware devices are located inside the computer or laptop, and they include the **CPU and RAM** *(Computer hope, 2021)*.

App

The full word for 'app' is 'application'. Apple gives this name to programs that you install on Mac OS X and iOS devices. However, other programs are pre-installed and therefore cannot be deleted.

MacOS and its Update

The operating system of Macs is called **macOS**. All new Macs have the latest version of Apple's advanced operating system called **macOS Monterey**.

App Store

An App Store is a digital store where Apple sells applications for Mac OS X and iOS. It can also refer to Apple programs on each of the platforms that permit you to gain access to the stores. Once you get access, you can buy, pay for, then download the applications.

Apple Store - apple.com

Apple Music

You can listen to over 90 million songs using a streaming service called Apple music. With this service, you are able to download tracks that you like and then play them offline, if you wish. In addition to listening to original and exclusive music, it's possible to get lyrics in real time and listen across your favorite devices.

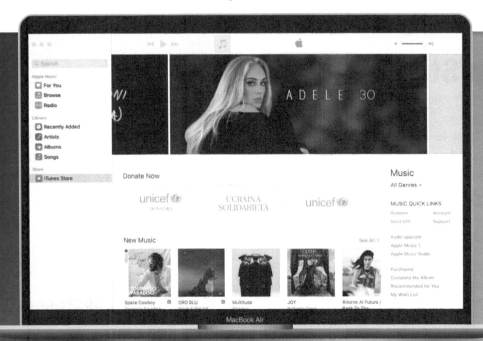

Apple Music on MacBook

Apple ID

An Apple ID is an account that you can use to make purchases from the Apple Store. Apple IDs can also be utilized to get other Apple services such as Find My iPhone and iCloud. To set up your Apple ID, go to **Settings**, then select **iCloud** in iOS and **Settings**. Afterward, go to **iCloud on Mac OS X**.

iCloud

This refers to a range of services that are offered by Apple. Some of the outstanding features of iCloud include calendar sync, push email, and iTunes Match. Your iCloud is accessible on the go.

Browser

This application program provides you with a service that makes it possible for you to look for and interact with information on the **World Wide Web (WWW)**. You get this information by entering query words in search engines, as a way of specifying what you are looking for. Considering the wide variety of information that is available over the internet, this is important. Some of the information that you can get through browsers includes images, videos, as well as Web pages. When using the WWW, you are able to navigate through information, thereby reading the specific text you wish to know about. The term 'browser' originates from the functionality of enabling you to navigate through information on the WWW. Many people see the browser as a necessity for accessing the internet, thereby making it one of the most used tools on the computer.

On behalf of the user, a web browser uses **Hypertext Transfer Protocol (http)** when making requests on Web servers throughout the internet. It is interesting to note that the first **Web browser** was created in 1990 and was called **World Wide Web.** Later on, the browser's name was changed to Nexus, so that confusion would be avoided with the developing information space called "the World Wide Web."

In 1993, Mosaic was introduced, the first web browser to feature a graphical user interface *(Tech Target Contributor, 2019)*. The Mosaic was followed by the introduction of Microsoft's Internet Explorer.

Home Page - Safari Browser

Common Features of Web Browsers

Most web browsers have common features. These features help to provide ease of use when it comes to using the Internet. We will look at these common features in this section.

- **Home button:** When you select a home button, you will be brought to a pre-defined homepage.

- **Web address bar:** This will allow you to input a Web address so that you can access the website.

- **Refresh:** A refresh button helps to reload a Web page, especially when it appears stuck.

- **Back and Forward Buttons:** These buttons will take you to move to the previous or next page.

- **Bookmarks:** These make it easier for you to select particular, predefined self-chosen websites.

- **Tabs:** Tabs serve to open multiple websites in an individual window.

- **Stop:** This is the button which stops a page from loading by making a web cease communication with the server.

Apart from the above-mentioned features, numerous browsers also provide plug-ins. These help to extend the capacity of the browser. For instance, plug-ins can enable you to perform tasks such as adding security features.

Back and Forward Buttons   Home Button

Refresh Button   Tabs

Web Address Bar   Stop   Bookmarks

Web Browsers Function

Web browsers function as part of a client/server model. The client, which is the browser that runs on your device, makes requests to the Web server. On the other hand, the server also transmits information back to the browser. Afterward, the browser construes and shows the information on your device.

Google Search Bar - www.google.it

Commonly Used Browsers

Currently, the most commonly used browser is **Google Chrome**. However, there are other browsers that people use as well. Let's get more details about various examples of browsers in this section.

- **Safari:** Safari is a browser that is used for Apple computers as well as mobile devices of the same brand.

- **Microsoft Edge:** This browser comes as a replacement for the Internet Explorer.

- **Firefox:** Firefox is a browser that was developed by Mozilla.

- **Opera:** This is a stable and fast browser. It is compatible with most operating systems.

- **Flock:** Flock is an open source browser that is based on Firefox. It is optimized for social bookmarking and blogging.

- **Lynx:** Lynx is a text-only browser for VMX and UNIX shell users.

Safari   Opera   Firefox   Flock   Edge   Chrome   Lynx

Storage

Storage is alternatively referred to as digital storage, storage medium, or storage device. A **storage device** is able to hold information on a temporary or permanent basis. Computers use two types of storage devices, which are primary storage devices such as RAM and secondary ones like the hard drive. The secondary storage can be external, internal, or removable.

To date, you can store computer data on three types of media. These three forms of **data storage** are **optical, magnetic, and solid-state storage** *(Computer hope, 2021)*.

An example of **magnetic storage** is the **hard drive** and that of an **optical storage** device is a **CD-ROM disc**. The third type, which is the solid-state storage or flash memory, replaced most optical and magnetic media because it is more reliable and efficient, in addition to being cheap. Examples of **solid-state storages** include **USB flash drive, CompactFlash, memory card, SD card, and Sony memory stick.**

Storage of data can also be done on paper, though this method is no longer popular. You could also store your data online and on the cloud. Online and cloud storage is currently becoming the order of the day because it allows you to access your data from more than one device. It is also possible to access your data on the go. Moreover, if your computer is stolen or damaged, you won't need to worry about losing your data if you use cloud or online storage. You will simply access it and load it onto your new device.

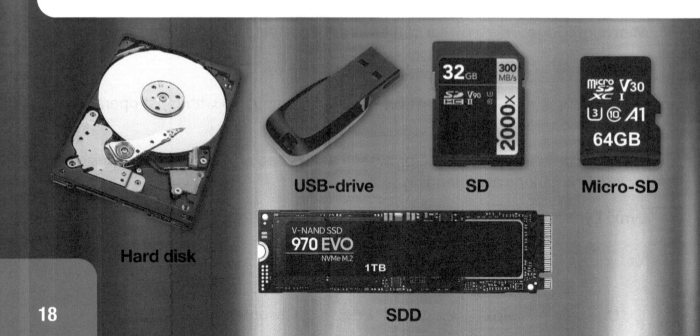

Hard disk   USB-drive   SD   Micro-SD

SDD

Siri

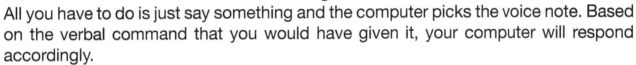

Siri is a voice-recognition technology. It allows you to perform a lot of functions on the device without having to use the touchscreen.
All you have to do is just say something and the computer picks the voice note. Based on the verbal command that you would have given it, your computer will respond accordingly.

Sleep or Wake Button

This is the button on your device that is used to switch it on or put it back into an inactive state. By holding it down, you can entirely power down your device. In some instances, **the Sleep or Wake button** is also called the **Power button** *(Fry, 2022)*.

Power Button

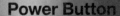

Gigabyte/GB

GB is an abbreviation for **'gigabyte'**, which is a measurement for data storage for smartphones, tablets, computers, gaming consoles, as well as other computing devices. There are 1024 megabytes in a single gigabyte. Depending on size, you can store 3000 ebooks or between 5000 and 15000 documents in a gigabyte *(West County Computers, 2017)*.

Hard Drive - 500GB

System Preferences

The **System Preferences** is a native application, and it allows you to adjust a lot of things in the system of your device. This may include switching data for Wi-Fi on or off, changing the desktop wallpaper or particular settings for other applications. The system preferences icon looks like a load of gray gears. This application is quite handy because it gives you the leverage to customize some aspects on your computer, thereby making the latter more enjoyable to use.

Gestures

These are a set of movements done by fingers in order to interact with touch screen devices. **Common gestures include 'flick', tap, pinch, and unpinch.** The flick gesture is characterized by swiftly moving your finger in a downward or upward manner. It is usually used when you want to scroll up or down a web page. Sometimes used when you want to move through a long list of items. The tap gesture is the same as clicking with your finger.

Another gesture, the pinch, is the movement of the pinching finger and the thumb. This is usually used when you want to zoom in on items. Lastly, the unpinch gesture is the opposite of the pinch. This gesture is used for zooming out.

Attachments (On Mail)

An **Attachment** is a file that is sent together with an e-mail message. It can be a Microsoft Word document, picture, sound file, movie, Excel Spreadsheet, or any other form of file. Attachments may include computer viruses, worms, trojans, or other malware. It is, therefore, wise for you not to open an attachment unless you are expecting it from someone whom you know. The standard icon for the attachment is a paper clip *(Computer hope, 2020)*.

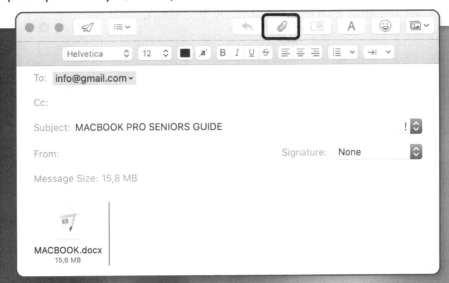

Desktop

A **Desktop** is commonly used to refer to a system unit. However, the graphical user interface or operating system mainly refers to the way icons are organized on a screen *(Computer hope, 2020)*. In this sense, the desktop shows icons for your Internet browser, Recycle Bin, and Task Bar, just to mention a few.

It is also possible to create shortcuts on the desktop to increase the ease at which you can access certain pages, documents, applications, or information.

Icon

An icon is a minute graphical representation of a file, feature, or program. When you click or double-click the program that is represented by an icon, the program will open. In other instances, a certain action occurs.

For instance, the icon may be highlighted. Icons are a component of GUI operating systems such as Microsoft Windows and Apple macOS X. They assist users to quickly identify the type of file that is represented by the icon.

Dock - Icons Apps

Lightning

Apple gives this name to the **connection port** on its laptops, desktops, or phones. The connection port is used to connect to the mains for charging. It can also be connected on other computers for syncing and charging purposes.

Lightning - Connection ports

Wi-Fi

Wi-Fi is a wireless technology that is used to transmit data to a mobile device from a router. Some of the mobile devices that can use this technology are tablets, smartphones, and laptops. Wi-Fi makes it possible for you to access the internet without having to connect through internet cables. The latest wireless technology is Wi-Fi 6. With Wi-Fi technology, you can even use the data on your phone for accessing the internet on other devices such as your laptop.

All you have to do is click on the **internet network icon** on your laptop and enter the password that is associated with the Wi-Fi on your phone. This whole process is known as hot spotting. So, be sure to switch on the hotspot on your phone before you can make attempts to connect your computer.

Wi-Fi / Internet Network icon

Cellular

Cellular is a **network technology** that enables mobile device communication over areas that have transceivers and cells. The transceivers and cells are also known as cell sites or base stations.

In a cellular network, commonly used mobile transceivers are cell phones or mobile phones. Cellular technology enables mobile device users to carry out a number of tasks such as message transmission, placing calls, Facebook updates, and Web browsing.

4K - Ultra HD

It is named as such because it stands for 4000, referring to 4000 horizontal pixels. This is a new type of monitor and television that is expected to replace high-definition technology.

The most common one has a resolution of 3840x2160 pixels, which is four times larger than that of a high-definition television set.

Due to this technology, it is possible to edit a 4K video on a Mac Pro, which would be very demanding when it comes to other laptops that are not updated to this level.

3D Touch

This is a new **touchscreen technology** that was put forward by Apple when they launches iPhone 6s and 6s Plus. The 3D touch refers to sensitivity due to different amounts of pressure that can be exerted on a gadget. Simply put, depending on how hard you press, you could activate different functions on your Apple device.

The **Apple 3D touch** allows you to swipe or push on the screen with more pressure so that you can preview various types of content. You could also specifically access application functions from the home screen.

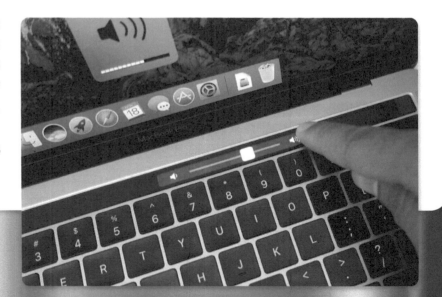

Touch Bar

CPU

The **central processing unit (CPU)** is responsible for handling all instructions that come from the hardware and software as the computer runs. Other names for the CPU are processor, central processor, or microprocessor. Although the CPU is mainly referred to as the computer's brain, it is rather proper to denote software as the brain, while the CPU is addressed as the efficient calculator.

This is because the CPU is exceptionally good when it comes to numbers. However, without the software, the CPU would not have the know-how of doing anything else. **Two primary components in the CPU include the arithmetic logic unit (ALU) and control unit (CU)**. The ALU carries out logical, mathematical, and decision operations, while the CU directs all operations of the processor *(Computer Hope, 2021)*.

GPU

GPU stands for graphics processing unit. The GPU is crucial for both business and personal computing. Despite being popular in gaming, GPUs have found many uses in artificial intelligence and creative production.

Originally, GPUs were meant for the acceleration of 3D graphics projection. However, as time progressed, the GPUs became more programmable and flexible, thereby improving their capabilities. The improved functionalities of GPUs led to the creation of more exciting visual effects and realistic acts that have shadowing techniques and advanced lighting.

Other developers also started to harness the power of GPUs to increase workloads in high performance computing and more. To date, GPUs are used for gaming, machine learning, video editing, and content creation.

RAM

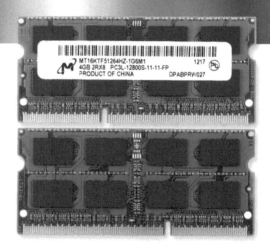

The random-access memory (RAM) is a hardware that facilitates the storage and retrieval of information on a computer. The RAM is also known as the primary, system, or main memory. In the RAM, data is accessed quickly in a haphazard manner, rather than sequentially. The RAM consists of volatile memory. Therefore, power is needed to keep the data accessible. In cases where the computer is switched off, all the RAM data gets lost.

A computer's performance is mainly dependent on the amount of memory that it has. A slower performance results if a computer does not have enough memory to run the operating system as well as its programs. If a computer has more memory, it is able to load additional information and software, thereby processing information at a faster rate.

IPS Tecnology

IPS stands for in-plane switching. It is a **type of monitor** that provides an improved color reproduction. Apple MacBooks, iPhone, iPod touch models, and iPads use **IPS displays**. This explains the incomparable color projection of these devices.

CHAPTER 2:

THE "MUST-KNOW" ASPECTS

The "Must-Know" Aspects of the MacBook Line of Laptops

After reading this chapter, you will have an enhanced understanding of the MacBook of your choice. We will compare and contrast the different types of MacBooks that are available. This knowledge is of paramount importance because it ensures that you make a good choice, especially when it comes to selecting the right MacBook for you.

MacBook Air

MacBook Air is the lightest and thinnest notebook that is powered by the M1 chip. As Apple's first system on a chip, the M1 chip has security features, the processor, GPU, I/O, and RAM all in just one chip. Please note that the M1 chip was custom-made for Mac. This silicon chip is very small, though extremely efficient as compares to Apple's previous chips. This is because the chip is built on a five-nanometer processor.

The MacBook was updated in November 2020, and it starts at a price of $999 *(Charlton, 2022)*. It has a 7 or 8-core GPU, an 8-core CPU, and a 16-core neural engine for machine learning. There are two models of the MacBook Air, each 13.3-inch with 2560 x 1600 display. The first one, which goes for $999 has the M1 chip with 7-core graphics and a storage of 256 GB. The other one costs $1,249 and contains the M1 chip with 8-core graphics and a storage of 512 GB.

One of the first Apple mac laptops to make a shift to Apple silicon was the MacBook Air. After the transition, the MacBook Air now had a slim, fanless design, overly enhanced performance, and an improved battery life.

The battery life of MacBook Air is quite impressive. It will provide you with up to 18 hours of video playback and about 15 hours of surfing the internet when you are using the Apple television application. A new and updated version of the MacBook Air is expected to come out in 2022 *(MacRumors, 2022)*.

Other laptops have a fan for cooling purposes. However, the **MacBook Air contains an aluminum heat spreader that disperses heat**, thereby permitting silent operation. Compared to the older models of MacBook Air, the aluminum heat spreader stands as the only internal change that has been made to it. Since Apple does not use Intel processors, but its own custom silicon for the MacBook Air, it is more likely that the laptop will be updated more regularly in the future.

Most of the previous updates to MacBook Air were internal, instead of external ones. The laptop continues to have a tapered, aluminum body that is wedge-shaped. Its other feature is a **13-inch Retina display with thin bezels**. In addition to that, it has a large **Force Touch Trackpad.** You will find the MacBook Air in silver, gold, and space gray.

The 13-inch screen has a new P3 wide color support that enables the projection of more vivid and real colors. It provides a true tone that enhances a strategic match between the screen's white balance and the ambient lighting. It allows for a more natural viewing experience, thereby cutting down the chances of eyestrain. This laptop supports a brightness of up to 400 nits *(Apple, 2018)*. **MacBook Air has a magic keyboard that contains a refined scissor mechanism.** These features offer up to one millimeter key travel that allows for a more stable key feel.

The MacBook Air laptop has a 720 pixels facetime HD camera that works with the **M1 chip** to enhance picture quality, reduce noise, and offer an improved dynamic range. The MacBook Air's keyboard is slightly tweaked to further promote ease of use. Apple has added function keys such as "Spotlight search," "Do not disturb," and dictation options. Also included on the keyboard is a new "emoji Fn key."

The keyboard also has backlit keys that are controlled by an ambient light sensor to allow them the ability to light up in dark rooms. MacBook Air also has exceptional security features. Instead of using your password, you could use your touch ID fingerprint sensor when you want to unlock your Mac or make purchases. The touch ID is protected by the Secure Enclave, which functions to keep your personal information and fingerprint data safe.

The MacBook Air functions with Wi-Fi 6 or 802.11ax and Bluetooth 5.0. It has two Thunderbolt 3 or USB 4 ports that allow up to a 6000 external display. MacBook Air contains stereo speakers that have wide stereo sound support, a 3.5-millimeter headphone jack, and a three-microphone array *(Apple, 2018; Charlton, 2022)*.
Here is a quick summary of the current specifications of **MacBook Air:**

- **13-inch screen size**
- **8 or 16 GB of RAM**
- **2560 x 1600 retina display with true tone**
- **Up to 2 TB SSD**
- **Apple M1 chip with 8-core CPU**
- **Apple M1 chip with 7 or 8-core GPU**
- **Thunderbolt 3/USB 4**
- **Scissor-switch magic keyboard**
- **Touch ID**

MacBook Pro

In 2016, Apple introduced two models of the **MacBook Pro** *(Moreau, 2019)*. One was with a touch bar, whereas the other had none. The updated MacBook Pro without a touch bar completely replaced an earlier version of MacBook Air. It had a lighter and thinner chassis. The MacBook Pro with a touch bar was priced at $2399, while the one without was going for $1499.

The MacBook Pro with a touch bar was more advanced than the one without. The touch bar dynamically adapted to each active application and substituted the row of old-fashioned function keys. Incorporated on the touch bar was a **Touch ID sensor**. Thunderbolt 3 or USB-C ports, a second - generation butterfly mechanism keyboard, trackpad, and a brighter, wider gamut display were available on the new MacBook Pro.

The other changes to the MacBook Pro included enhanced speakers with improved dynamic range, a notably faster PCIe-based solid state drive, and a new color, space gray.

The MacBook Pro has a uniform, slab-style design. It also has ventilation as well as fans. This laptop runs faster than the MacBook Air, thereby making it perform harder, and longer, with an enhanced performance overall. The high performance is made possible by the ability of the MacBook Pro to run at higher temperatures. These temperatures are efficiently cooled by its active cooling system.

Although the difference in performance is not very large, it is better for you to use MacBook Pro if you prefer an **improved performance**. The MacBook Pro comes with a **standard 8-core GPU** *(Newsroom, 2020)*. For a lot of graphics-based work, MacBook Pro is the best choice. It costs only $50 more when compared to the 8-core GPU model of the MacBook Air.

The MacBook Pro has a 13.3-inch backlit display that contains **IPS technology, P3 wide color, and true tone**. All these features are similar to those of the MacBook Air. Therefore, the colors and content will be relatively the same on both devices. However, the brightness of the MacBook Pro can reach up to 500 nits. This points to the fact that the MacBook can be 20% brighter. If you prefer a brighter display, it is best to go for the MacBook Pro.

The battery life of MacBook Pro extends up to 20 hours *(Charlton, 2022)*. As we mentioned earlier, the MacBook Pro has a uniform, slab-style design and is able to house larger batteries. This results in the prolonged battery life that it has. Consider using the MacBook Pro for excessive video content consumption or if you prefer listening to music using the built-in speakers.

The MacBook Pro comes with a touch bar. The touch bar uses a **"Retina quality" multi-touch display**. An interesting aspect about the touch bar is that its controls change depending on applications that you are using. For instance, the touch bar allows easy access to emoji in Messages and offers a simple way to scrub through videos or edit images. In Safari, the touch bar is able to show Favorites and Tabs.

MacBook Air vs MacBook Pro

SIMILARITIES

The similarities between the MacBook Air and MacBook Pro include the following:

- A 13.3-inch LED-backlit display with **IPS** technology.

- Eight-core **M1 chip with 16-core Neural Engine and up to 8-core GPU**.

- **Magic keyboard.**

- **Touch ID.**

- **Bluetooth 5.0.**

- **Two Thunderbolt / USB 4 ports.**

- **Up to 2TB of storage.**

- **Up to 16GB unified memory.**

- **802.11ax Wi-Fi 6.**

DIFFERENCES

The differences between the MacBookAir and MacBook Pro include the following:

- **The MacBook Air has a slim, wedge-style, while the MacBook Pro has a thicker, slab-like design.**

- **MacBook Air comes in space gray, silver, and gold. The MacBook Pro is available in silver and space gray.**

- **MacBook Airs weight 2.8 pounds, while MacBook Pros weigh 3.0 pounds.**

- **MacBook Air reaches a brightness of up to 400, whereas MacBook Pro goes up to 500 nits.**

- **The battery life of MacBook Air extends up to 18 hours, while**

• Support for Dolby Atmos playback and wide stereo sound.

MacBook Air

MacBook Air

that of MacBook Pro reaches 20 hours.

• MacBook Air has a passive cooling system compared to the passive one that is found on the MacBook Pro.

• When it comes to stereo speakers, MacBook Air has simple ones. Contrastingly, you will find a high dynamic range of stereo speakers on the MacBook Pro.

• MacBook Air is configurable with up to 8-core GPU, while a standard one is available for MacBook Pro.

• The MacBook Air has a simple three-microphone array with directional beamforming, whereas that of MacBook Pro is more enhanced, since its studio quality.

• MacBook Pro has a touch bar, which is not available on the MacBook Air.

iMac

Apple introduced the **new iMac** (inspired by the best of Apple) in April 2021, which is an all-in-one desktop computer. The recent iMac features an entire redesign, a 24-inch 4.5K display, and enhanced performance through the exceptional M1 chip (MacRumors, 2021). It comes in a range of fun colors that include blue, pink, green, silver, purple, yellow, and orange. Its accessories, such as the magic mouse, keyboard, power cord, lightning to USB-C cable, and the magic trackpad, also have the same color as the iMac.

The matching keyboard could have a number pad or it may not have one. Some models have a built-in Touch ID on the keyboard. The magic keyboard has a wireless Touch ID implementation. It utilizes a keyboard security component to communicate with the Secure Enclave so that purchases can be made and unlocking easier.

The iMac contains a 8-core CPU with four high efficiency cores. It also has four high performance cores, together with an 8-core integrated GPU. When compared to the previous iMac 21.5-inch model, the 24-inch one provides a CPU performance that goes up to 85 times faster, three times faster machine learning capacity, as well

as double the GPU efficiency (Apple, 2022g). The RAM reaches up to 16 GB.

The thinner design is made possible by the incorporation of the M1 chip. Thermals and the logic board have been greatly consolidated, thereby enabling the iMac's reduction in size. It, therefore, fits easily in various places because it now takes up less space. Due to the new cooling system and thermals of the M1 chip, iMac has become quieter. The thickness of the computer is 11.5 millimeters. Also present is a slim stand that has been redesigned to allow adjustment of the display angle. A new magnetic power connector powers the iMac, and its color matches that of the available woven cable. There are softer pastel colors at the front of the machine. However, the back has much bolder and brighter colors.

The screen has a resolution of 4480 x 2520, 500 nits brightness, and 11.3 million pixels. This computer has more than a billion colors, P3 wide color, and true tone (Amazon, 2021). The true tone allows for a more natural view by matching ambient lighting to the color temperature of the display.

Also included on Apple's iMac is a 1080p FaceTime HD camera that has a new image signal processor. Consider a situation when you want to take a photo but the lighting is not good. With iMac's image signal processor, you are able to capture great photos in low light. The Neural Engine incorporated in the M1 chip permits better noise reduction, enhanced white balance and auto exposure, as well as greater dynamic range. When it comes to sound, the iMac has a six-speaker sound system that has clear mids and highs, together with a strong bass (Hanson, 2021). The machine supports Dolby Atmos and spatial audio. It also has studio-quality microphones.

Wi-Fi 6, the fastest possible Wi-Fi performance, is supported by iMac. The storage capacity can be customized with about 2TB of SSD. At the back, iMac has two thunderbolt 3 or USB-4 ports that allow super quick transfers of data. This permits customers to connect to various external devices. For some models, four USB-C ports are also found at the back.

On its side, it has a 3.5-millimeter headphone jack, and the **machine supports an external display of up to 6K.** The higher-end model has an ethernet port in the power adapter. This helps in allowing a cable setup that is less cluttered.

Here is a summary of the current specifications of **iMac:**

- It is 11.5 millimeters thin.
- It contains the revolutionary M1 chip.
- It possesses a 24-inch, 4.5K retina display.
- Seven bright color options are available.
- It has a touch ID keyboard.
- It also includes color matched accessories.
- It has enhanced microphones, webcam, and speakers.
- Its pricing starts at $1299.

CHAPTER 3:

THE BASICS OF THE MACBOOK

This chapter will focus on the basics of the MacBook. It will provide you with a step-by-step guide on how to use your MacBook. In addition to the steps that enhance the ease at which you use your Mac, troubleshooting tips are also offered. With such information, correcting discrepancies in the way your device functions will be easier than you can ever imagine. Let's get started!

The First Startup and Main Configuration

Setting up a new Mac is easy and straightforward because you only need to follow the on-screen instructions to get off to a good and exciting start.

To set up your new Mac, press the **"power button"** to switch it on.

After that, **choose a language** that your computer will use across the system, be it English, French, or Spanish, you name it. Click Continue.

Then select the **keyboard layout** that you prefer.

After selecting the keyboard layout, there are other things that have to be set up as well. These include **network options**, **location services**, **Apple ID**, and the **time zone** based on your current location.

Depending on the amount of storage that you have on your device, you could also store your iCloud documents on your new Mac. Remember to click **"Enable Siri on this Mac"**, your computer's personal virtual assistant.

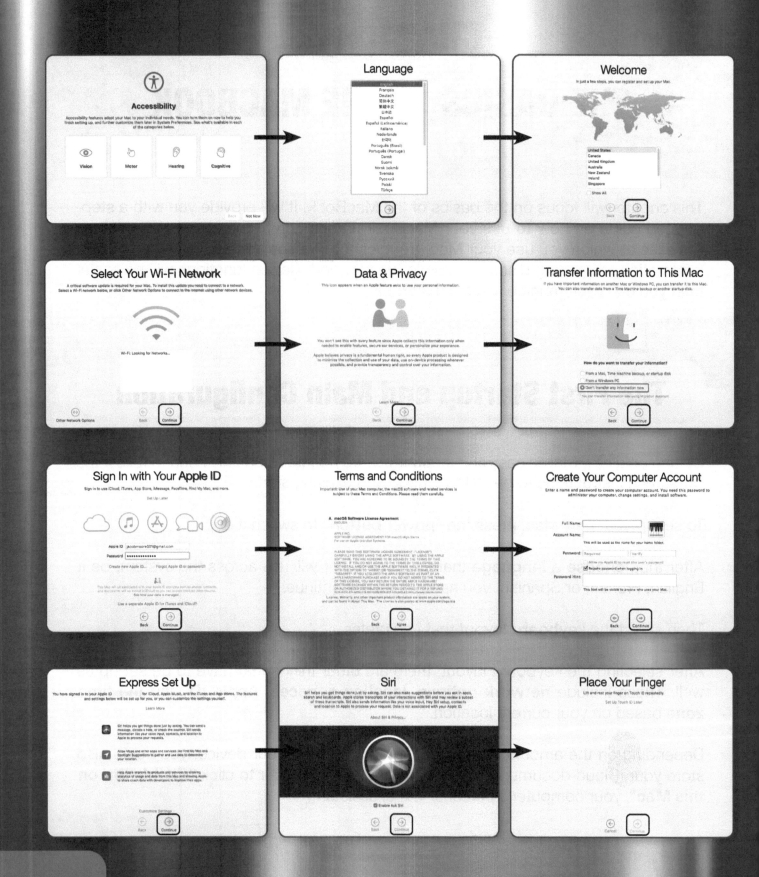

Your Mac will then finalize all settings. This may take some time, but it's worth your while. It is normal for you to see a spinning wheel and an on-screen message which says **"Setting up"** *(Chan and Wolfe, 2021)*.

Login Screen and Touch ID

To use the **Touch ID** on your MacBook, put your finger on the fingerprint scanner when you are prompted to do so by an on-screen message. When logging in to your MacBook or if you want to use Apple Pay, you can touch the fingerprint scanner. It is important to set up the Touch ID on your MacBook before you start using the Touch ID feature *(Laukkonen, 2021)*.

To **set up Touch ID on your MacBook**, go to the Mac menu bar and click the **Apple icon**. In the drop-down menu, choose **System Preferences**, then select **Touch ID.** Click **Add Fingerprint and put your finger on the Touch ID key** upon being prompted to do so. Do a repeated series of lifting and repositioning of your finger on the Touch ID.

As you keep doing this, your fingerprint begins to register on the screen in red.

If you continue repositioning your finger on the Touch ID key, the entire fingerprint will turn red.

This means that a complete impression has been reached and be sure to click **Done** when this happens.

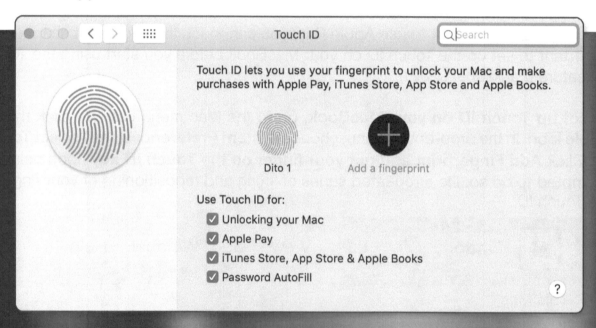

Connecting to Wi-Fi Network

To connect to **Wi-Fi** using your MacBook, go to the **menu bar** and click the **Wi-Fi icon** 📶. After clicking the Wi-Fi icon, go ahead and **select a network from the menu**. You might be asked to enter the network's password prior to joining the network. In some cases, you may be asked to agree to terms and conditions (*Apple, 2022b*).

There is another way to go about it if you do not see the Wi-Fi icon in the menu bar. Simply select **Apple menu** , then go to **System Preferences**. Afterward, click Network. On the sidebar, choose Wi-Fi, then select Show Wi-Fi status in menu bar.

If you want to connect to a Wi-Fi network that is hidden, select Other Networks or **Join Other Network** from the Wi-Fi menu, then select Other. Afterward, provide the requested network name, security, as well as password information.

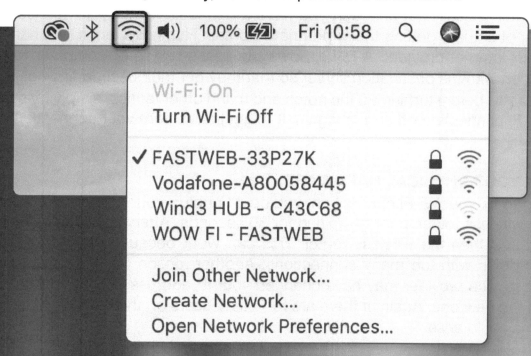

Troubleshooting Your Mac's Wi-Fi Connection

There are a number of solutions that you could try if your Mac doesn't seem to connect to Wi-Fi. At times, your connection may apparently just drop out for no reason. Your Wi-Fi connection might drop out because of issues to do with hardware in your home or the computer. Other issues may arise from software on your computer. Another possible reason is issues that are associated with your service provider. Let's discuss the possible solutions that you could try in this section.

ENSURE THAT THE WI-FI CONNECTION IS THE CORRECT ONE

Sometimes Macs skip from the desired Wi-Fi connections and connect to another network instead. This usually happens if there are available 'open' networks that do not necessarily provide an internet connection. That could be the source of your connection problem.

In some cases, you might see the Wi-Fi symbol with an exclamation mark in the middle. This means that although you have a connection with your wireless router, you are not actually getting the appropriate Domain Name System (DNS) handshake from your internet provider. A DNS allows the user's laptop or computer to have a connection with the destination server so that they get their desired findings (Halliday, 2010). Lastly, before turning up the notch and trying other tactics, simply try switching your Wi-Fi connection off and on again. It might just restore your connection back to normal.

CHECK YOUR PHYSICAL HARDWARE

In trying to fix your Wi-Fi connection, you could unplug your cable modem as well as your wireless router, prior to waiting for 30 seconds. Afterward, plug in your cable modem and then the wireless router. This can work because your router may be bogged down with too many connections. Another reason could be because your internet service provider may have changed your IP address and your router fails to pick up the new one. Again, if there are too many users on the network, connectivity problems could arise.

CHECK YOUR SYSTEM UPDATES

If you are running a beta version of OS X, check if there are no pending system updates that you have not installed yet. Upgrade to the latest vanilla version of the operating system if the Wi-Fi is giving you problems. There might just be bug fixes that will do away with your problem.

HOW ABOUT CHANGING YOUR DNS SETTINGS!

It is possible that your Wi-Fi is working fine but the internet access is not there because your internet service provider's DNS is not functioning in a proper manner. In instances such as this, it is advisable to use a **free public DNS**, of which Google has a remarkable one.

To access Google's public DNS, open Network Preferences from System Preferences or from the Wi-Fi icon 📶 **in the top menu bar.** Click **Advanced.** Select DNS from the menu option and hit the plus icon. Afterward, add one of Google's DNS addresses, either 8.8.4.4. or 8.8.8.8. Click **OK** and start browsing on the Internet again.

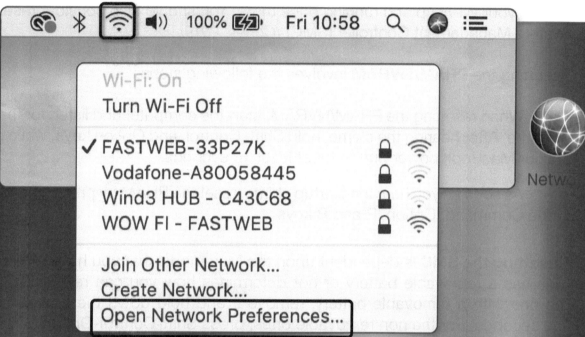

CONSIDER RESETTING NVRAM/PRAM AND THE SMC

Even when the device is turned off, two internal Mac components, NVRAM (Non-Volatile Random-Access Memory) and PRAM (Parameter Random-Access Memory), store the memory. This is utilized in places such as the internal clock of your computer. Resetting the PRAM or NVRAM can efficiently clear out virtual cobwebs, thereby getting your Wi-Fi up and running once more. You should also consider resetting the System Management Controller (SMC) *(Curley, 2019)*.

Resetting the **PRAM/NVRAM** involves the following steps:

- When resetting the PRAM/NVRAM, start the computer and listen for the startup chime. After hearing the chime, hold Shift, Control, and Option keys, while pressing your MacBook power button for at least 10 seconds.

- As soon as you hear the startup chime, reset the PRAM by pressing and holding the Command, Option, P, and R keys.

Resetting the SMC is dependent upon the Mac model that you have. Whether your Mac has a removable battery or not determines how you can reset the SMC. For the one with a removable battery, remove it and hold down the power button for five seconds. For the non removable ones, press Shift-Control-Option and the power button. Hold these for 10 seconds, then release.

CHECK WIRELESS DIAGNOSTICS

Apple has incorporated a built-in Wi-Fi troubleshooting tool that it has improved over the years. For you to access the Wireless Diagnostics tool, search for it in the Spotlight search function. Alternatively, follow the next set of instructions.

- In the status menu at the top of your screen, **hold down the Option key and click the wireless icon**.

- From the dropdown menu, choose **Open Wireless Diagnostics**...

- A pop-up window will be displayed, from which you will select **Monitor my Wi-Fi connection and click Continue**.

You will then be presented with a detailed look at your network options. The computer will provide you with a series of steps in a bid to help you to identify and give solutions to your Wi-Fi problems. If this doesn't help, it's time to set up Wireless Monitoring so that your Mac gathers information on your persistent problems.

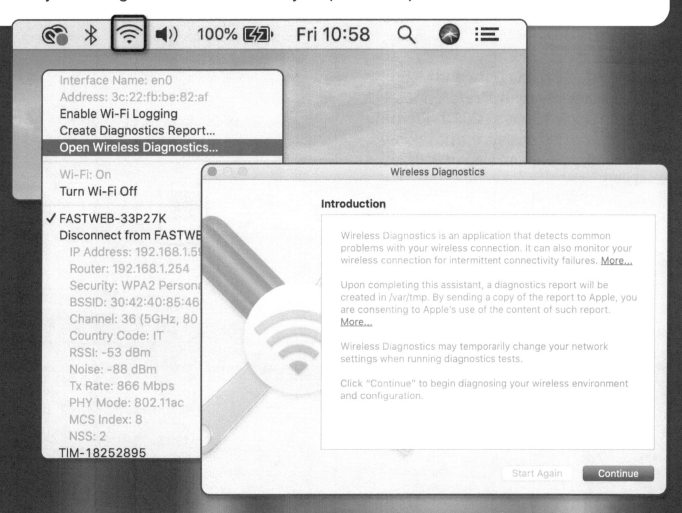

RESTART YOUR MAC

If you have tried everything but it's not working, restart your computer. Although it is the oldest trick in the book, you may just get the response that you are looking for. However, if it doesn't work, and you have exhausted every other option, your connection problems may be hardware-related. It could be your computer or the router that is problematic.

Customizing the Dock and Menu Bars

The Dock is a minute panel that allows you to quickly access your folders, files, and recently used applications on your Mac *(Hellotech, 2020)*. There are changes that you can make to your Dock as well as your Menu Bar if you do not like the way it appears on your Mac.

To customize your Dock and Menu Bar, click **System Preferences**, then Dock *(Sellers, 2021)*. From here, you can change the position, magnification, and size of your Dock.

You can also add and remove folders by dragging them to and from the Dock and Menu Bar.

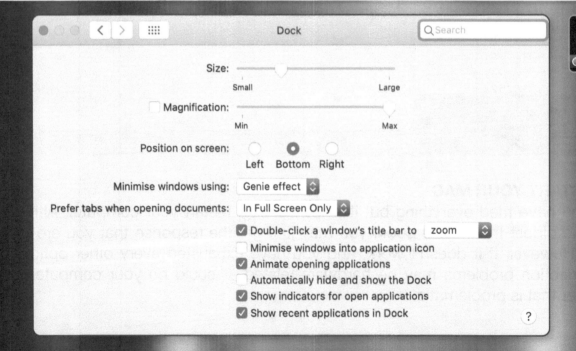

Using Safari to Navigate the Internet

Safari combines the address and search bars for navigating the Internet and conducting the searches, respectively. It combines these two into one bar, which is called the Smart Search Field. Suggestions for websites as well as search items are provided by the Smart Search Field, thereby making it easy to surf online *(Apple, 2022f)*.

When it comes to navigation, Safari uses three main buttons, which are the Back, Forward, and Refresh ones. The Back and Forward buttons permit you to move through pages that you have just viewed earlier. To see your recent history, you can click and hold either button. The Refresh button reloads the current page in cases where the website has stopped working. Sometimes, the Refresh button may act as the Stop button. This happens if a webpage does not load correctly.
See more details on page 19 "Commonly Used Browsers".

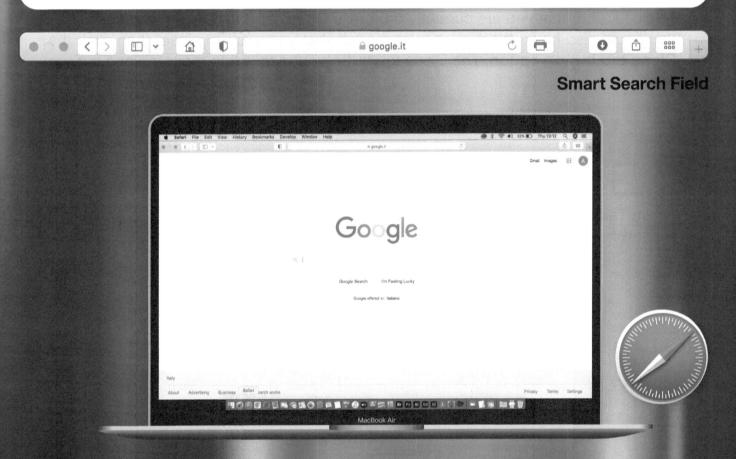

Smart Search Field

Home Page - Safari Browser

Opening Windows and Tabs on Safari

When you want to view different pages on new windows, Safari allows it. Safari also allows you to use an individual window when you want to open multiple websites using tabs.

Click **File**, then choose **New Window** when you want to open a new window. Alternatively, press **Command** and **N** on your keyboard.

In the top-right corner is the new **tab button**. Click this to open a new tab. Alternatively, press **Command** and **T** on your keyboard.

By default, the new tab will appear as favorites. **To navigate a new page, simply type an address and press Enter.** The page will then open in a new tab.

To close a tab that you are currently on, press **Command** and **W** on your keyboard. You could also hover the mouse over the tab that you want to close, then click the **Close tab button option**. The Close tab button appears when more tan one tab are open.

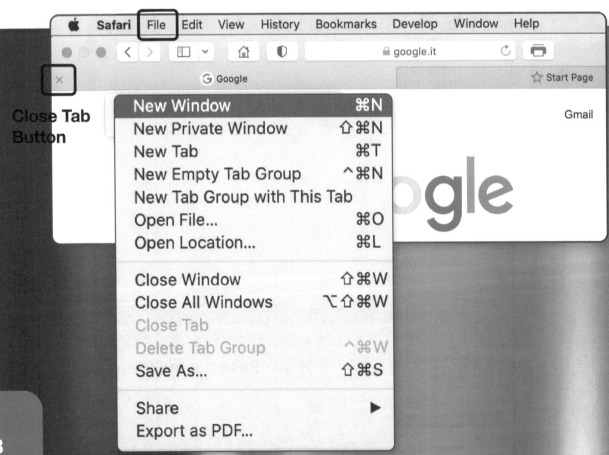

Close Tab
Button

Browsing History

Safari is able to keep your browsing history, which is a record of the websites that you visit. Safari enables you to search your history when you want to find a previously viewed page. For the sake of privacy, Safari also allows you to delete your history.

To view your browsing history, click **History**, then choose **Show All History**. Your history will open in a tab, and it shows your **recent browsing history**. On the top of the page, you will find the most recent history because the list is sorted by date. If you are interested in revisiting a site, just double-click the link (gcfglobal.org, 2021).

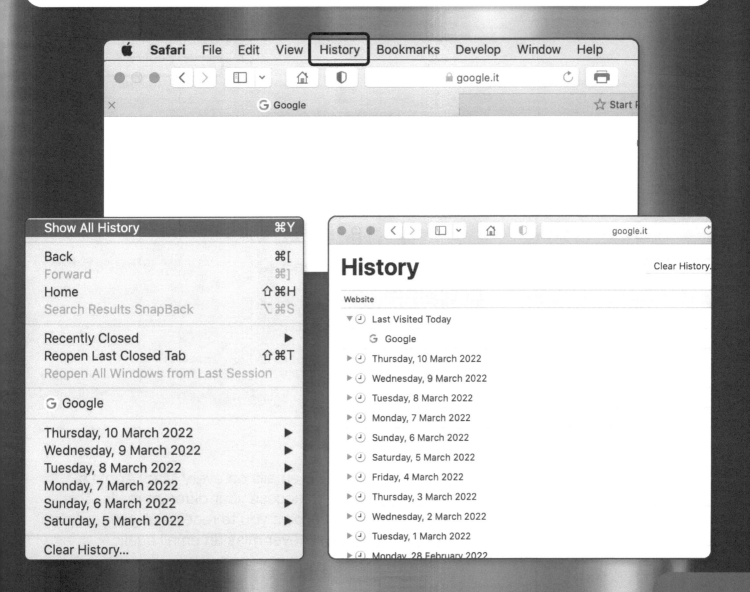

Downloading Files on Safari

A file may **download automatically** if you click its link. However, due to differences in file types, it may simply open within the browser. To prevent a file from opening in Safari, use Save Link As to directly download it to your computer.

To download a file, **right-click, then choose Download Linked File**. The file will start downloading and the progress of the download will be shown on the top-right corner of the browser under the Downloads button. Once the download is complete, double-click the file to open it.

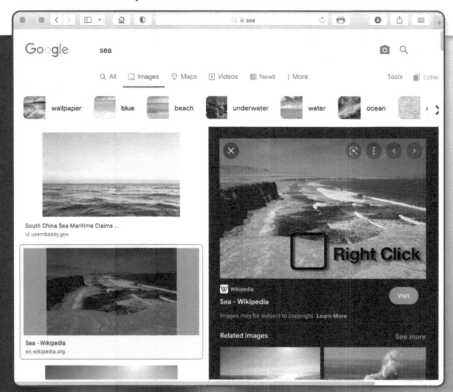

Adding an Email Account

You will find Mail, which is Apple's app for sending emails on every Mac. Apple's Mac is a great alternative to use when you want to access your different mails. This is because it is possible to set it up in a way that allows you to receive all your emails from various email accounts in one place. You will never miss an email again.

To find the Mail app on your Mac, click on the Mail icon in the Dock.

You could also press **Command** and **Space Bar**, then type in **'Mail'**. Open **System Preferences**, then click on **Internet Accounts**. A list of commonly used services such as iCloud, Google, Facebook, and Yahoo will appear on the right. Click on the **+ sign** if you do not see these, then add an email to Mac *(Haslam, 2020)*.

You could also add an email account from within Apple Mail. Open Mail, and then go to the menu, click on Mail, and choose Accounts. This opens the same screen that you get through System Preferences. Then add an email to your Mac.

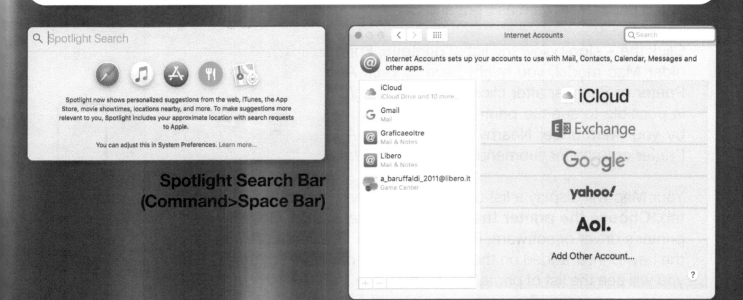

Spotlight Search Bar
(Command>Space Bar)

Adding a Printer to a Mac

There are numerous ways to connect a printer to a Mac. It can be through a **wireless connection, IP address, USB, or WPS**. You can do a wireless connection through a Bluetooth or Wi-Fi Protected Set-up (WPS).

Let's discuss more details on how to add your printer to a MacBook in this section.

ADDING A PRINTER THROUGH WPS

A connection via WPS usually requires you to press the Wi-Fi or Wireless button on your printer, then the WPS button on your router. Please note that steps may vary depending on the type of printer or router that you have. Therefore, you should check for specific instructions on your router and printer guides. Once you manage to set up WPS, you can progress using the following steps.

On the top left corner of your screen, click the **Apple icon** . Afterward, go to **System Preferences** and click on **Printers and Scanners**. If you are using an older version of Mac, the option for Printers and Scanners is found under Hardware as Print and Scan.

Click the **+ sign** below the list of printe\rs. For an older Mac model, you might have to click Add Printer or Scanner after clicking on the + sign. It is possible to see the printers that are detected by your Mac under Nearby Printers in the Add Printer or Scanner submenu *(Hellotech, 2021a)*.

Your Mac will display a list of discoverable printers on the network under the Default tab. **Choose the printer that you would like to add.** Go to Use field and select the printer's driver or software. Finally, click **Add**. The list of printers will be updated, with the new printer added on the list. On the left-hand side of the Print and Scan window, you will see the list of printers available.

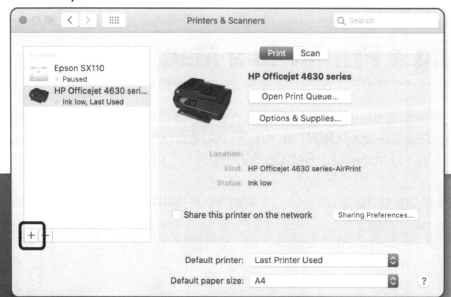

Printers & Scanners

ADDING A PRINTER THROUGH THE USB
To add a printer via the USB, plug your printer's USB into your Mac desktop or laptop. Click the **Apple icon** and go to **System Preferences.**

Afterward, click **Printers and Scanners**. Then, below the list of printers, click the **+ sign**. Choose a printer to add. The Default tab will give a list of printers that are available on the network. Then, **look for a printer name with USB** listed under the column for Kind.

Afterward, click **Add** and the printer will be added to the list of printers. The list is there on the left-hand side of the Print and Scan window.

ADDING A PRINTER THROUGH THE IP ADDRESS
You need to know your printer's IP address if you want to add a printer using this step. To find the IP address, click the Apple icon, then go to **System Preferences.**

Click on **Printers and Scanners**. Below the list of printers, click on the **+ sign.** Click on the **IP icon,** which looks like a blue globe icon. In the Address field, type your printer's IP address. Your Mac will then collect information about the printer. You can rename the printer, if you wish. Select the print driver that you want to use in the **Use field and** click **Add.**

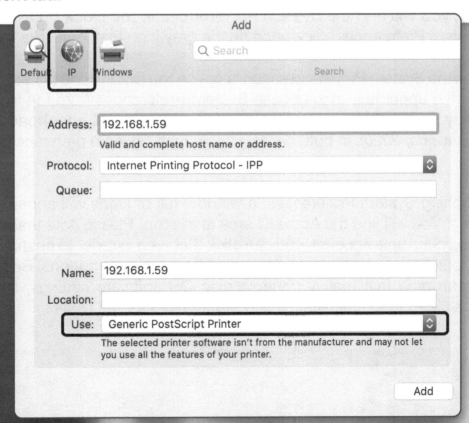

CHAPTER 4:

LET'S START WITH THE BASICS TOGETHER

In this chapter, we continue looking at the basics of a MacBook. We are going to learn how to do certain tasks and to use certain applications. Let's get further into the nitty-gritty!

Control Center

The MacBook's equivalence to the Control Panel is the **System Preferences.** Windows refers to its configuration options as settings, but mac OS calls them 'preferences'. Before you change any preferences, you first have to launch the **System Preferences Application.**

By default, you will find the System Preferences in the Dock on every Mac. To launch System Preferences, click once on the gray icon that looks like a gear.

Sometimes the System Preferences icon is not on the Dock. For a faster way to launch it, click on the upper left, then choose System Preferences from the list. **You could also quickly launch System Preferences by using either Launchpad or Spotlight Search** (Edwards, 2020). In both cases, simply type "system preferences," then click Enter.

Upon launching System Preferences, a window full of icons will appear divided into four regions. You will find the Apple ID area at the top. Please note that if you are signed into your Apple account, you can click that area in order to change your iCloud settings, personal account information, as well as payment options. Below the Apple ID area is an area that mainly controls mac OS software settings, including your desktop, background, notifications, and preferences for the Dock.

These options are involved in how the operating system functions. The next divider comprises of preferences that are linked to your Mac's hardware such as your mouse or trackpad, display, audio in and output, as well as Bluetooth *(Winters, 2020)*. Additional preference icons are seen at the bottom. These control third party applications, such as Adobe Flash. Any icon that you see in the "Additional preference" region was installed by an application and is not originally part of mac OS.

To change a certain preference, simply locate the one you want to change and click it. This will result in a shape change of the preferences window, thereby allowing new settings to appear. The forward and back buttons that are in the toolbar at the top of the window are used to navigate through System Preferences.

To see the whole list of preference icons once more, click the Icons button that contains 12 black dots *(Edwards, 2020).* In cases where you do not know where to find a certain setting, simply use the Search bar at the upper right, then look for the preference of choice in System Preferences.

For more details on system preferences go to chapter 8, pag. 117

Desktop

Have you ever been in a situation where your files are jumbled up all around the desktop? It is important to note that an organized file system is critical when it comes to keeping your digital life easier on a Mac *(John, 2019)*.

Although **Mac has a remarkable search feature that helps you to find files,** there are times when you can't remember a file name or maybe you may not have given an appropriate name to the document. A particular document may simply read "untitled document". As such, it becomes even more difficult to find what you are looking for.

There are a number of ways to **make a new folder on a Mac**. You could **create a new folder using Finder**. To create a new folder via Finder, **go to File and select New folder** in the Finder menu. This folder will appear wherever you are in your Finder file tree.

You could also create a new folder using a trackpad or mouse shortcut. Simply two-finger tap your trackpad or right-click your mouse from your desktop or in the finder file system to bring up a menu. The first option is "new folder." With this option, you are able to create a new empty folder wherever you are in the system.

Another way to create order out of desktop chaos is to use the **File section.** This is usually used for sub-folders. **Go ahead and choose multiple files that would be contained in a new folder that you created from trackpad or mouse shortcuts mentioned above.** This new folder should suffice to house most of the sub-folders that would have been cluttered on your desktop.

Spotless App.

Another great way to manage your files is to use the **Spotless application**. When using Spotless, you can simply **drag and drop your files onto the application's pop-up drawer that is in your Menu bar.** With Spotless, you can set the rules to sort your files and never again worry about organizing your desktop.

In addition to that, Spotless allows you to create a schedule for organizing files on your desktop according to what you prefer. This way, the application will automatically organize random files. Spotless is even more interesting in that you can set it directly send some items to Trash if need be *(Setapp team, 2020)*.

How to Copy, Cut, and Paste

When you want to cut, copy, or paste the text into a document, follow the instructions that we will describe in this section. **The first step is to highlight the text that you want to cut or copy.** If you are utilizing a trackpad or mouse, **position the cursor at the beginning of the text** that you want to copy.

Afterward, click and hold while dragging the cursor over the text that you want to copy. In cases where you are using a keyboard, position the cursor at the beginning of the text that you want to copy. After that, press and hold Shift while using the keys to select the text that you want to copy. Upon completing the highlighting process, a colored box will appear around the selected content *(Fox, 2021)*.

To copy the highlighted text, press Command plus C on the keyboard. You could also select **Edit**, then **Copy** from the menu bar. To cut the text, press **Command** and **X** on the keyboard. Also, you could go to the menu bar and choose **Edit**, then **Cut**.

To paste the text that you just cut or copied, position the cursor in an editable area, be it in a document or a text box. Press Command and V on the keyboard or select **Edit**, then **Paste** from the menu bar *(Hellotech, 2021b)*. Please note that if you want to copy cell contents in Excel, select the cell but not the text, then copy it.

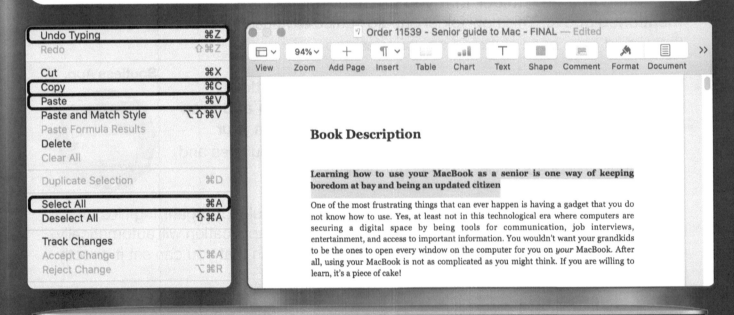

Other Keyboard Shortcuts

There are other keyboard shortcuts that you can use when it comes to copying and pasting commands. Depending on your cursor position or selection, there is a keyboard shortcut that highlights all items or text that is in the current view.

To select all, press Command and A on your keyboard. The Select All command comes in handy when you have to copy a whole document. Another keyboard shortcut, **Command and Z, helps to undo your most recent action.** This works well when you have just pasted text in an incorrect location *(Fox, 2021)*.

Copying and Pasting an Image

Select an image by dragging the cursor over it, then select **Copy Image** from the **menu.** When you do this, the image goes on to your clipboard.

You can now paste the image into any field that accepts them using the steps that we described in the previous section.

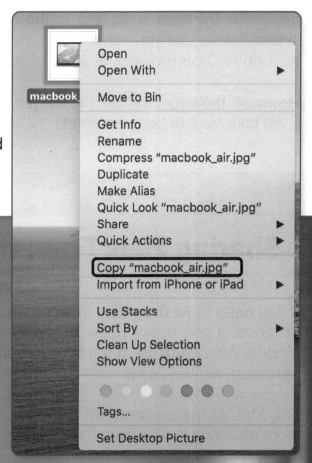

Using AirDrop to Share Files with Another iOS Device

One of the most convenient ways to transfer content or files from one Apple device to another is AirDrop. AirDrop allows you to quickly share videos, photos, documents, audio recordings, notes, web links, and contact cards between Apple devices.

Take note that **AirDrop is limited to Mac OS and iOS only.** For content to be shared between these devices, both of them must be within a 30-feet range from each other.

Both should also have their **Bluetooth and Wi-Fi functionalities turned on.** Currently, there is no limit to the size of the file that you can transfer through AirDrop *(Holland, 2022)*.

However, the larger the file, the longer it will take for it to be transferred.

Sharing Files From the iPhone to Mac

If you need to **AirDrop files from an iPhone to a Mac,** begin with the content. For instance, if you desire to AirDrop a web link, have the page already open on your iPhone. Afterward, go to the **Share menu and tap on the AirDrop icon.** Select the Mac icon, as well as the name of the device that you intend to send the web link to.

The Mac of the recipient will display a prompt requiring them to Accept or Decline from receiving the file from the other device

Upon tapping Accept, the transfer will begin.

When the transfer is complete, the link can be opened in the default web browser of the receiving device.

If you want to AirDrop files from your iPhone to

your Mac when both are signed into the same Apple ID, it becomes even easier. You will not see an option to accept or decline. The transfer is automatic in such cases.

Changing Your AirDrop Name on iPhone

Having an AirDrop name is similar to possessing a general device name. To change or check it on an iPhone, go to **Settings**, tap **General**, and then **About**. A list will appear, of which the first item displays the current name of your iPhone. **Just tap on it to change it.**

Troubleshooting AirDrop Problems

AirDrop has been around for quite a while now and has been subject to updates. Even though it has been updated, problems can still come up. Let's take a look at some of the ways to troubleshoot problems that may arise when you are using AirDrop in this section.

• **Your iPhone may not appear as an AirDrop destination.** If this happens, ensure that your personal hotpsot is turned off. To do this, go to Settings, then Personal Hotspot. AirDrop relies on Wi-Fi and Bluetooth; therefore, an interference with either, or a separation of more than 30 feet between devices, can lead to poor performance as well as an adverse effect on reliability.

- **Your Mac may not appear as an AirDrop destination due to an inactive Wi-Fi.** Ethernet may not be sufficient. Also check the Mac's firewall activity. If it is active, it might have been set to stop incoming connections.

For you to correct this issue, go to **System Preferences**, choose **Security and Privacy**, then **Firewall. Click the lock to make changes.** Enter the password or Touch ID if your mac requires it.

Under Firewall is Firewall options. **Deselect** by clicking **Block all incoming connections**.

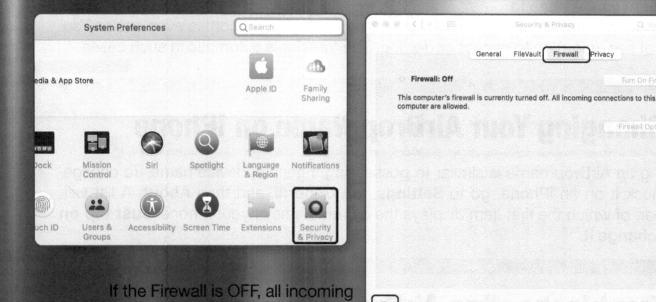

If the Firewall is OFF, all incoming connections are allowed.

- **For the best results with AirDrop,** ensure that you are using the latest versions of mac OS, iOS, and iPadOS, together with recent Apple hardware.

- **You may be asked to accept transfers between your own devices.** This means that the devices are not logged in to the same iCloud account.

- **There are cases where you can't find a file that has been sent** in the destination Downloads folder of Mac because it has retained its original modification and creation dates. It may be sorting differently than expected.

Using Airplay to Stream Content

Apple users are able to use Airplay on their television for watching videos, while playing from their Macs or any other Apple device.

To stream a video, connect your device to the same Wi-Fi network as your Airplay 2-compatible smart TV or Apple one *(Apple, 2022p)*.

After that, find the video that you want to stream, then click the Airplay icon. The last step should be to select your **Airplay 2-compatible smart TV or the Apple one.**

When you are done enjoying your videos and you want to stop streaming, simply click the Airplay icon in the application that you are streaming from, then tap your Mac from the list. Please note that some TV manufacturers have directly incorporated AirPlay 2 into their TV sets. This means that you can mirror or share just about anything from your Mac device to your AirPlay 2- incorporated smart TV *(Wall, 2022)*.

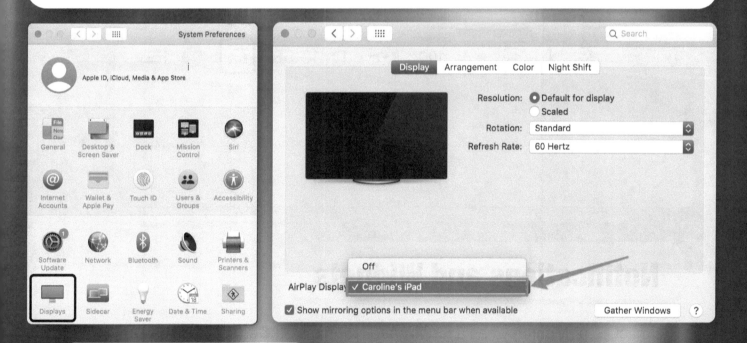

Using Spotlight

Regular use of your Mac for work and personal life may cause you to have lots of folders, photos, or files all over your computer. **Spotlight enables you to search your Mac for just about anything**. This implies that Spotlight will make it become easier for you to find whatever you need. When compared to searching in your Finder, Spotlight does more than just scanning your computer for downloads and saved files. It goes on to search the Internet for weather, news, and other content that is linked to what you are looking for *(Wolfe and Filipowicz, 2020).*

To use the spotlight search on your Mac, click the magnifying glass icon that you find on your top menu bar in the upper right corner. You could also press **Command and the space bar on your keyboard to launch the shortcut.** Type your desired phrase or word into the search bar. Spotlight will show you the relevant downloads, emails, messages, and documents that are on your computer.

In addition to that, Spotlight will utilize the Internet to reveal related web sites for your search items and dictionary of definitions, whenever possible. If need be, Spotlight will also show other pieces of information such as entertainment and weather. To view more, or get more details on a certain subject, click on any search result that will have come up *(Perino, 2020).*

Notifications and Widgets

The macOS 12 Monterey has a redesigned **Notification Center. It is now an individual column with notifications and widgets in the same place.** To access this Notification Center, go to the menu bar on the screen's upper right and click on the date. If you click a notification, you will be taken to the corresponding application. For example the Messages application will open if you click on a Messages notification. In cases where you have multiple notifications from an application, they will be grouped together. For instance, if your News alerts are active, there will be categories of news outlets. Upon clicking one, the category will expand so that you can view all the notifications *(Loyola, 2020)*.

You will find the widgets under the notifications. These are simple and minute items that offer **quick access to controls or information.** While other widgets show information that has been gathered from the Internet, most of them are of Apple applications such as Reminders, Podcasts, and Calendar.

Click on the date and time to open the notification center.

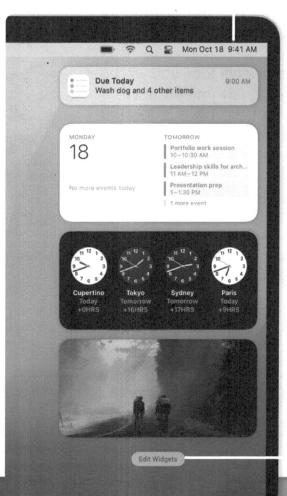

View notifications you haven't seen.

Customize widgets.

Talk to Siri

Siri provides you with the ability to interact with Things through speaking. Just make a request and Siri will do it for you *(Broida, 2013)*. For instance, if you want to be reminded to buy milk at 11 a.m., you can simply create a task by saying, "In Things, remind me to buy milk at 11 a.m."

With this application, you are able to add tasks, show lists, and have it read things to you.

Please note that **Apple's Siri requires certain syntaxes and functions better with some phrases compared to others.**

With this exceptional tool, you will be able to efficiently communicate with your machine. Let's have a look at some of the phrases that work best with Things.

• Instead of "to do," you can say 'task'.

• In place of 'tag', 'project', or 'area', say 'list'.

• Remember to start or end with "with Things" or "in Things." Otherwise, your tasks will be handed to your task Reminders application.

Use Handoff Between Your Devices

Have you ever wondered if it is possible to start work on one device and pick up where you left off on another? With Apple's Handoff, this functionality is very possible. **You can only use Handoff functions when your devices are close to each other.** Each of the devices must be signed in with the same Apple ID on iCloud. Also, be sure to turn on the Wi-Fi, Bluetooth, and Handoff *(Mishra, 2021)*.

To turn on Handoff on your Mac, select the **Apple menu** , then go to **System Preferences.**

Click General and choose Allow Handoff between this Mac and your iCloud devices. On an iPad, iPod touch, or iPhone, go to **Settings**. Select **General**, then **Airplay and Handoff. Turn on Handoff.**

Applications that work with Handoff include Maps, Reminders, Safari, Mail, Contacts, Calendar, Keynote, Numbers, Pages, as well as many third-party applications. To use Handoff, start performing a tas such as writing a document.

Proceed on your other device. **If you are switching to your Mac, go to the Dock and click the application's Handoff icon.** If you are switching to your iPod touch, iPad, or iPhone, open the App Switcher and at the bottom of the screen, tap the app banner *(Apple, 2021c).*

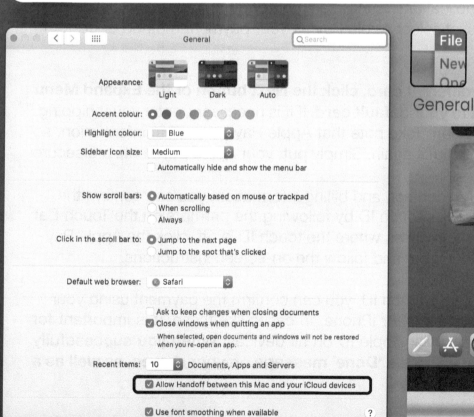

Use Apple Pay to Buy Something

To set up Apple Pay on your Mac, go to Wallet settings and click to add a card on more and follow the instructions.

Make sure that when you do the setup process, you verify your information with your card issuer or bank.

When using a Mac with a touch ID, go to System Preferences, then Wallet, and Apple Pay. Once you add your card to your wallet, you are all set to make payments using Apple Pay. Within applications or in Safari, **you can utilize Apple Pay to make payments** *(Apple, 2021)*. Just select Apple Pay as your payment method or click the Apple Pay button.

If you want to pay with a different card, click the Next button or the Expand Menu option that appears next to your default card. If it is necessary, enter your shipping, contact, and billing information. Take note that Apple Pay keeps that information, so there is no need for you to input it again. Simply put, your Apple payments are secure

After entering your shipping, contact, and billing information, you can confirm the payment using your MacBook's touch ID by following the prompts on the Touch Bar and placing your finger on it. In cases where the touch ID is off, click the Apple Pay icon that appears on the touch bar and follow the on-screen instructions.

For a Mac that does not have a touch ID, you can confirm the payment using your Bluetooth-connected Apple Watch or iPhone. In cases like these, it is important for you to be signed in with a similar Apple ID on all devices. **When you successfully complete a payment, you will see a 'Done' message on your screen, as well as a checkmark.**

Here are some of the **advantages of using Apple Pay**:

• Apple Pay utilizes sophisticated technology to encrypt and protect each transaction that you do.

• Apple Pay payments are also protected by touch ID. Therefore, even if your phone is stolen, your information will be locked down.

• Apple Pay payments are fast. Each transaction takes only a few seconds.

• Convenience is another plus when it comes to Apple Pay payments. You are always able to pay for what you need even if you leave your wallet at home. *(Squareup, 2021).*

CHAPTER 5:

INTERNET & APPS

Internet and Apps to Stay in Touch With Your Loved Ones

After reading this chapter, you will be equipped with knowledge on how to use Apple devices on the internet. You will also learn how to use some applications that help you stay in touch with your loved ones. Not only will you learn how to communicate with them while seeing their faces on the gadget, you will also attain the know-how with regard to speaking with them using messages. Let's get more information on how to go about using your Mac to start and maintain connections with the people who matter to you.

Using Safari

There are many web browsers that you can use to stay in touch with your loved ones. In addition to Safari, there is Google Chrome, Opera, and Mozilla. However, the best way to enjoy the internet on your Apple devices is to use the Safari browser. Safari outperforms many other browsers in terms of how it functions.

To make Safari your default browser on a Mac, select the **Apple menu** , choose **System Preferences**, then click **General**. Afterward, a pop-up menu will appear, from which you should click the Default Web Browser option, **then select Safari** *(Apple, 2022j)*.

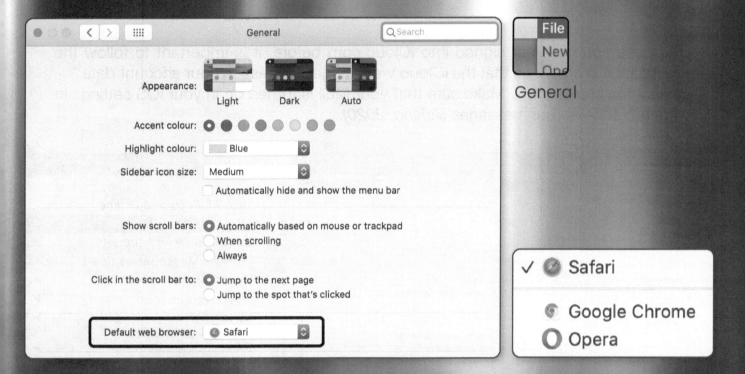

Checking Your Email

In Mac Mail, the quickest way to manually check for new email messages is to press **Command, Shift, and N on your keyboard.** Another way is to click on the **File on Mailbox menu and then select Get All New Mail.**

There is yet another way that you can use to access your iCloud email on a Mac; open your **Finder,** click **Applications,** then select **System Preferences**. Sign in with your Apple ID, username, and password, if prompted. Otherwise, you may need to double-**click the Apple ID icon.**

Click the blue box that is next to the Mail option, in case it has not been selected. Afterward, close the System Preferences window, then click the **Mail App icon in your Dock.**

It is also possible to **check your iCloud email on the iCloud Website**. The first step is to **visit iCloud.com**. Afterward, sign in using your username and password.

Suppose you have not signed into iCloud.com before, it is important to follow the verification prompts so that the iCloud website gets access to your account data. Select the Mail symbol. Make sure that your Mail is turned on in your iOS settings in order to access your messages *(Ariano, 2020)*.

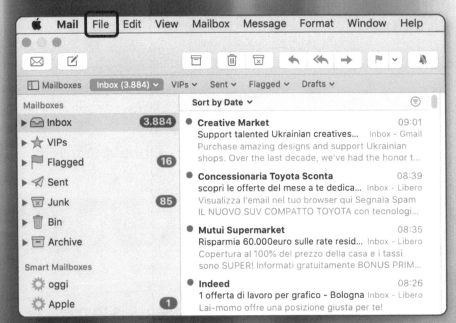

Chatting Using Messages

It is possible to send unlimited messages to any iPod touch, iPad, iPhone, and Mac using Apple's secure-messaging service called iMessage.

To send a message, open Messages. After doing this, you might be asked to **sign in with your Apple ID.** You can then click the **New Message button**, which you will find at the top of the Messages Window.

To be able to send messages to the recipients, type their name, phone number, and email address. Alternatively, you could click the **Add button** and choose recipients from your list of contacts.

To type your message, press Tab or go to the bottom of the window and click the message field.

If you want to include an emoji, image, or audio recording, there are ways to go about it. For example, if you want to include an audio recording, go to the Record audio button and then say your message. Go ahead and click the Emoji Picker button if you wish to include an emoji. Press Return in order to send the message.

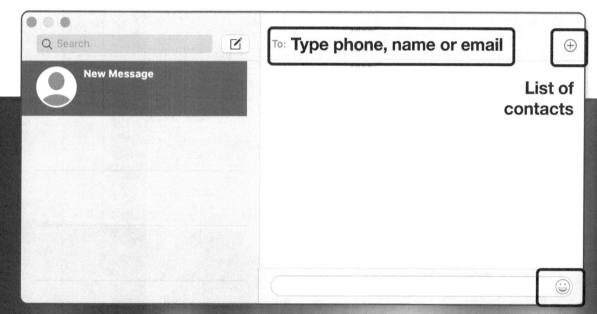

List of
contacts

Emoji Picker

Starting a FaceTime Call From Messages

When you are in a conversation with an individual or a group, it is feasible to start a FaceTime call. **FaceTime is an application that allows you to make voice and video calls over the internet.**

It is a great application for keeping in touch with your loved ones who use Apple devices.

On the upper-right corner of the window, in macOS Monterey, click the FaceTime button and select **FaceTime Video or FaceTime Audio**. You could also go to the upper-right corner of the window and click Details, prior to clicking the FaceTime audio or video button *(Apple, 2021e)*.

Customizing the Group or Your Information

You can change your name and photo by selecting **Messages**, then **Preferences** from the menu bar. Settings that allow you to edit your photo and choose whether or not to share your name and photo with others are available.

By **selecting the group conversation** in the sidebar and **clicking Details** in the top right corner of the window, **you can customize the group**. Click Change Group Name and Photo if you wish.

If you want to **remove a person from a group** of four or more members, **Control-click their name**. Afterward, select **Remove from Conversation.**

In cases where you **want to be excused from the group**, click **Leave this Conversation.** Sometimes, you may want a certain individual to be part of the conversation. **To add** them, simply **click Add Member.**

Deleting a Conversation or Message

Please note that **when you delete a conversation or message, you cannot get it back**. This is because the action is permanent.

However, if you feel that you need to **delete a message**, start by **selecting it**, choose **Edit**, then **click Delete from the menu bar.**

In case you want to delete a conversation, go to the **sidebar** and **Control-click it.** Select the **Delete Conversation option from the shortcut menu**, then click **Delete again in order to confirm the action.**

Making a Call With FaceTime to Other iOS Devices

It is interesting to note that with advances in technology, you are now able to receive or make a phone call in an area with little or no cellular coverage.

All you have to do is **connect to a Wi-Fi network**. To place Wi-Fi calls from your iPhone, turn on Wi-Fi calling in Settings. Click on **Phone**, then **Wi-Fi calling**.

In the status bar, you will see the option Wi-Fi after your carrier name if the Wi-Fi-calling service is available.

Please note that when there is cellular service, your iPhone utilizes it for emergency calls. In cases where you turn on Wi-Fi calling and the cellular service is not available, emergency calls might use Wi-Fi calling.

Adding a Device

Ensure that when you want to add a device, it should have the latest software version. To add other devices, **go to Settings on your iPhone, then turn on Wi-Fi Calling.**

Afterward, **turn on Wi-Fi calling on Other Devices**. Tap Add Wi-Fi Calling For Other Devices. The next step is to **go on your other devices and sign in** to iCloud and FaceTime with the same Apple ID and password that you utilize on your iPhone.

TROUBLESHOOTING TIPS WHEN YOU ARE FAILING TO ADD A DEVICE

- Ensure that you are using the same Apple ID for iCloud and FaceTime on your iPhone and the other device.

- Make sure that your devices have updated software.

- On your iPhone, ensure that you Allow Calls on Other Devices and Wi-Fi Calling are turned on and that your device is showing under Allow Calls On.

TURNING ON WI-FI CALLING FOR OTHER APPLE DEVICES

When using your iPod touch or iPad, **go to Settings, then FaceTime**. Afterward, **go to Calls from iPhone and tap Upgrade to Wi-Fi Calling**.

If you want to turn on Wi-Fi calling using your Mac, open FaceTime and select it.

Afterward, go to **Preferences**, then **Settings**, and choose **Calls from iPhone**. Last, **select Upgrade to Wi-Fi Calling**. Once you see a six-digit code, enter it on your phone, prior to **tapping Allow**. When calls on other devices are enabled, Wi-Fi Calling turns on automatically on your Apple Watch.

PLACING A WI-FI CALL FROM YOUR IPOD TOUCH, IPAD, OR MAC

To place a Wi-Fi call from your iPod touch, iPad, or Mac, make sure that your device is added.

Open FaceTime and tap Audio. Enter a phone or contact number, then tap Wi-Fi call. Alternatively, you can also make a call by tapping a phone number in Mail, Contacts, Safari, and Messages *(unthsc.edu, n.d)*.

Removing a Device

Take note that you can remove one of your devices if you don't want it to use Wi-Fi calling.

On your iPhone, **go to Settings**, tap on **Phone**, then **Calls on Other Devices**. A list of devices will appear, from which you can **turn off Wi-Fi calling from the device that you wish to remove.**

If you intend **to switch off Wi-Fi calling on your Apple Watch**, go to the Watch App on your iPhone and tap My Watch. Also, tap Phone, then **turn off Wi-Fi Calling.**

Take a Selfie with Photo Booth

It is possible **to take a selfie with Photo Booth** using your Apple device. Let's talk more about the photo booth so that you have a general understanding of what exactly it is.

A Photo Booth can be described as a portable kiosk that is used for snapping pictures of you and your friends in front of a backdrop (inlightphotobooths, 2019). In simple terms, a photo booth could be described as an entertaining and easy way to create memories, thereby filling the silence at your event, be it a party, wedding or any other joyous moment. The booths are either exposed or enclosed, depending on the vendor you get them from.

Let's discuss more on how you can use your Mac to take photos. **It is possible for you to capture an individual or group of four photos on your Mac.** You can also **record a video** using the built-in camera on your machine. Another possibility is the use of an external video camera that is connected to your Mac.

To take a photo using an external video camera, ensure that it is connected to your computer. Also, make sure that the camera is turned on.

Go to the **Photo Booth app** on your Mac, and then to the **View Photo button**. Afterward, click the **Take Photo button** 📷.

If you want to take a **single photo**, go to the bottom left of the window and click the **Take a still picture button.**

For a sequence of four photos, click the **Take four quick pictures option.**

These four photos are also known as **"4-up photos"**. Finally, click on the **Take Photo** option .

Recording a Video Using Photo Booth

Sometimes you may be eager to let your loved one know exactly how certain events are unfolding. It is possible to capture important events when they occur. Consider a situation where a baby starts to have its first steps. Although a loved one may not be able to see this as it happens, a video recording will come in handy in making them also experience the joy of seeing their baby walk for the first time.

If you have to record a video using an external video camera, ensure to connect it to the computer. Do not forget to turn the camera on.

When using your Mac, go to the **Photo Booth app** and click on the **View Video button** .

Afterward, click the **Record Video button** . Sometimes, the Record Video button may not show. In this case, go to the bottom left and click Record a movie clip button. When you are done capturing your precious moment, click the **Stop button.**

Applying an Effect in Photo Booth on Mac

Photo Booth has functionalities for adding some fun effects to your videos and photos.

To apply effects on your Mac, go to the **Photo Booth app.** Click on **Take Photo or Record Video.** Afterward, on the bottom right, click on **Effects Button.** [Effects] To see the preview of the available effects, click the browse buttons at the bottom of the window.

Afterward, select and click the effect that you prefer. When you move the pointer over the image, a slide that has some distortion effects will appear *(Apple, 2022a)*. Go ahead and move the slider if you would like to see how the distortion can change the photo or video. You can then select the distortion that gives the changes that you are looking for.

If the effects do not look appealing to you, it is possible to do away with them so that the photo or video becomes normal again.

In the middle role of effects, select **Normal**, then click the **Take Photo or Record Video option**. When the recording is complete, click the **Stop button.**

Viewing Photos on Mac

On your Mac, go to the **Photo Booth app** and select a thumbnail. Click one of the photos to have a larger view when you are viewing a 4-up photo.

To view all four photos, click again on the photo that allows you to have a larger view.

In cases where you want to see a slideshow of the photos, select **View**, click on **Start Slideshow**, then utilize the controls at the bottom of the screen.

Using Photo Booth to Export Photos and Videos

If you want to use your videos and photos in other apps, you can simply export them. Video clips are exported as MOV files, while 4-up and single photos are exported as JPEG ones. In the **Photo Booth app** on your Mac, export a video clip or photo by **selecting the thumbnail.**

Afterward, select **File**, then **Export**. In the case of a 4-up photo, **choose the photo frame**, then **File**, prior to clicking **Export**. To export a non-effect photo, choose the thumbnail, then select File and Export Original.

In addition to exporting photos and videos, there are other ways to share them from Photo Booth. These include sharing through Messages, Mail, AirDrop, Notes, Reminders, and Add to Photos.

Still in your **Photo Booth app**, choose the **photo or video thumbnails** that you wish **to share. Click the Share button** 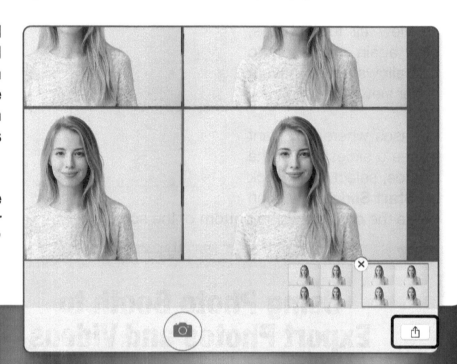 prior to choosing how to share them. If you choose Messages, for example, the photo or video will be inserted in a new text message.

If you choose to share your photos or videos through Mail, they will be inserted in a new email. AirDrop is another option for sharing. The Photo Booth app will list other people who are utilizing AirDrop. To share the files with them, simply click their names.

Choosing 'Notes' will make the photos and videos to be inserted in a new note, whereas the "Add to Photos" option adds them to your Photos library.

Photos and videos are inserted in a new reminder if you select 'Reminders' *(Apple, 2022)*.

CHAPTER 6:

PHOTOS AND MEDIA

In this chapter, we will focus on different actions that you can engage in as far as your photos are concerned. We will look at how you can alter your photos to create the outcome that you desire. Also included in this chapter are ways you can access various types of media that you can find on your Mac. Let's get more details on how to navigate through the photos and media on your Mac.

Viewing and Editing Photos

On your Mac, Photos allows you to rate, view, group, and store images. You can easily add photos to your iCloud library and sync them with all of your devices through iCloud. If you 'like' certain images in Photos, they are automatically added to your favorites. With its grouping feature, Photos makes it easier for you to find certain pictures when you need them. The **Photos app** allows for face detection. It allows you to see all the photos of a certain individual that are in your Mac *(Skylum, 2022)*.

Photo-editing tools can easily be used to make simple changes to your photos. Such changes include rotating them, as well as cropping them in order to get the best framing. There are also vast adjustments that can be made to change color and exposure, eliminate red-eye, change white balance, and remove blemishes or marks, just to mention a few.

It is possible to make further adjustments by using Levels and Curves controls to change contrast, brightness, and tonal range in different areas of the same photo. You can also change and improve videos and live photos.

APPLYING LEVELS ADJUSTMENTS TO A PHOTO

You can alter the settings levels to darken or lighten areas and **change the contrast in a photo**. It is possible for you to adjust settings for the shadows, highlights, mid-tones, and white and black points. The appearance of specific colors can also be changed.

To apply level adjustments to a photo on your Mac, **go to the Photos app, double-click a photo, and click Edit**. In the toolbar, click **Adjust**, then the arrow next to **Levels**. To automatically correct the adjustment levels of a photo, click the pop-up menu below Levels, select Luminance, RGB, or the color that you wish to alter.

Afterward, click **Auto**. To manually adjust levels, simply drag the handles of the histogram to make the desired adjustments. Option-drag a handle to move the bottom and top handles simultaneously.

THE DIFFERENT LEVELS AVAILABLE

Each of the levels mentioned in the previous section is different from the other. In this section, we will discuss how different they are. Let's get more details.

The Shadows level alters the darkness or lightness of shadows so as to reveal the desired details. Mid-tones alter the lightness or darkness of the photo's mid-tone areas. Highlights alter the highlights to your brightness of choice. The white point changes the level at which white areas are entirely white, whereas the Black point alters the latter to become completely black, up to the point where no detail is visible.

APPLYING CURVES ADJUSTMENTS TO A PHOTO

On your Mac, go to the **Photos app**, **double-click a photo**, then click **Edit**. In the toolbar, click **Adjust** and go to the **Adjust panel**, then **click the arrow next to Curves.**

To **automatically correct the curves of a photo**, click the pop-up menu below Curves. Select RGB or the color that you wish to correct. Afterward, click **Auto**.

To **manually adjust a photo's color curves,** click the **Add points option,** then click the areas on the photo that you wish to change. With each click that you make, points are added to the histogram's diagonal line. You can also add points by clicking along the histogram's diagonal line. Once you finish adding the points, drag the points to alter the contrast and brightness in the photo.

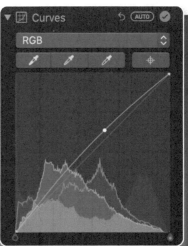

When you alter a video or photo, Photos preserves the original so that you can always undo your changes and return to the old, natural look. The alterations that you make to a video or photo will appear everywhere, be it in your library, project, or every other album in your Mac. Suppose you wish to give a photo or video an exceptional look that only appears in one version of the item, simply duplicate it, then work on the copy.

If you want **to edit a video or photo on your Mac**, go to the **Photos app** and **double-click a photo or video thumbnail.** Afterward, click **Edit** in the toolbar. Select a video thumbnail or photo, then press **Return**. The Edit toolbar shows a Zoom slider and buttons for making changes, cropping photos, adding filters, enhancing, and rotating photos.

To make adjustments to a photo, click Adjust. By clicking the adjust option, the adjustment tools will be displayed. From there, you can make the necessary ones that you wish to. Zooming in or out on a photo is done by dragging or clicking the Zoom slider.
To apply filters on a photo, click **Filters,** whereas **if you want to crop, select Crop** so that the cropping options are displayed
(Apple, 2022k).

Rotating a video or photo is done by clicking the **Rotate button in the toolbar.** Go ahead and continue clicking until you get your desired orientation.

To automatically enhance a video or photo, click the **Auto Enhance button** to get an **automatic adjustment** of the contrast and color.

If you wish to remove the changes, click **Revert to Original** or simply Press **Command and Z on your keyboard.** Once you finish the editing process, **click Done** or press Return *(Stavniychuk, 2021).*

DUPLICATING A PHOTO

As we mentioned before, if you want to create different versions of a video

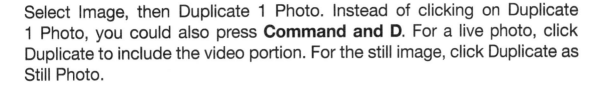

As we mentioned before, if you want to create different versions of a video or photo, you should first duplicate it. Afterward, you can then work on the copy. To duplicate an item on your Mac, go to the Photos app and select the photo you want to copy.

Select Image, then Duplicate 1 Photo. Instead of clicking on Duplicate 1 Photo, you could also press **Command and D**. For a live photo, click Duplicate to include the video portion. For the still image, click Duplicate as Still Photo.

COMPARING VIDEOS OR PHOTOS PRIOR TO AND AFTER EDITING

It is possible to make comparisons of the edited and original versions of an item. Using your Mac, go to the **Photos app** and double-click a video or photo to open it.

Afterward, **click Edit in the Toolbar**. To view the original image, press and hold the **M** key, or click and hold the **Without Adjustments button** ⬚⬚ . Release the **M** key or the button so that you can see the edited item.

COPYING AND PASTING ADJUSTMENTS

After adjusting a photo or video, you can copy the adjustments and paste them into other fields. Take note that the pasting of adjustments can only be done onto one item at any given moment.

On your Mac, go to the **Photos app, double-click an adjusted item**, and **click Edit in the toolbar. Select Image, then Copy Adjustments. Double-click the photo that you wish to apply the adjustments to, then click Edit.**

Select Image, then Paste Adjustments. Alternatively, you can Control-click an item in the editing view, then select Copy Adjustments or Paste Adjustments. Please note that you cannot copy and paste the settings from the red-eye tool, crop tool, retouch tool, or third-party extensions (Apple, 2022k).

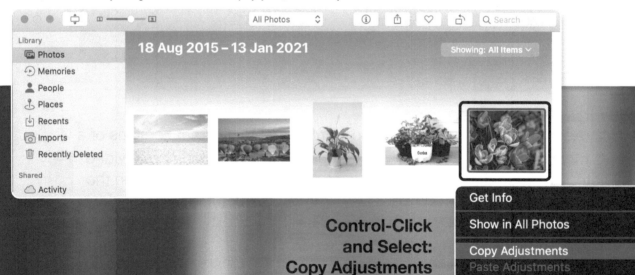

Control-Click
and Select:
Copy Adjustments

Listening to Music

In the Music app on your Mac, you can find music in your music
library. To find a particular album or song, click any option below
Library in the sidebar on your left. For instance, to view all the albums available in
your library, click Albums. To choose a playlist, go to the sidebar on the left and select
a playlist below Playlists. You can move the pointer over any song or album, after that,
click the Play button.

When listening to your music, it is possible for you to shuffle, repeat, play songs in a
particular order, fade between songs, and use the Playing Next queue *(Apple, 2022m)*.

USING THE MUSIC APP FOR MAC

The Apple Music part of the Music app is grouped into three key sections, which
are **Listen Now(or For you)**, **Browse**, and **Radio**. You can use the sidebar to navigate
through all of them.

From your Applications Folder or Dock, **open Music**. In the sidebar, click **Listen
Now** to see what your friends have been listening to, recently played playlists and
albums, as well as your Apple-curated mixes and suggestions. Still on the sidebar,
click **Browse to see currently-trending artists**, Apple's curated playlist selections,
new music, and the rest of Apple Music's available library.

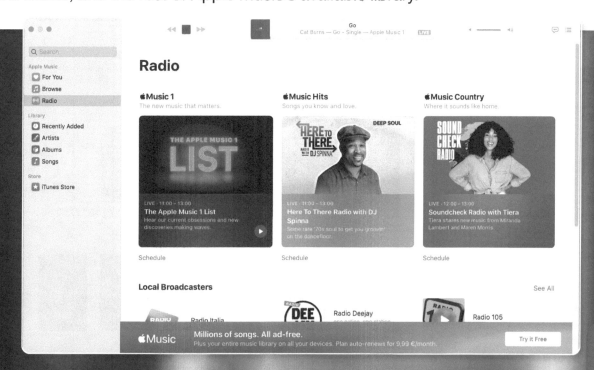

On the sidebar, you could also **click Radio to view and play Apple Music 1 radio shows,** both previously recorded as well as those who are live at any given moment. Click Music Country, Music Hits, or Music 1 in the Radio section to view and play content from those Radio stations **(Keller, 2021).**

IMPORTING MUSIC INTO THE MUSIC APP

To import music into the Music app, go to your Dock or Applications folder and open Music. In the **Menu Bar, click File, then Import.** Select the folder or file that you want to import and click Open.

Reading Books

Every Mac has **iBooks app** installed on it, which is designed to work well not only on your computer but across your Apple devices as well. This means that it is possible for you to read a chapter or two on your Mac, then continue from where you left off on your iPhone or iPad. **You can browse the iBooks store and download content to iCloud.**

The iBooks feature contains tools and themes that are similar to those on iBooks on iPad and iPhone.

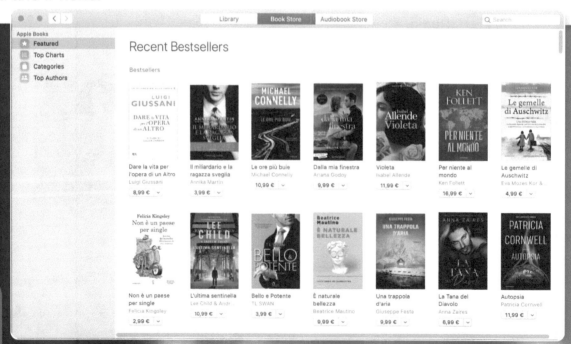

These features include style customizations, text size, color options notes, dictionary lookup, highlighting tools, voice-over, sharing, and illustration rendering.

Depending on your preferences, there are many other Reader apps that you can use on your Mac. You could use Kindle, Adobe Digital Editions, BookReader, and OverDrive Read. Let's get more details on how each of these functions in this section.

KINDLE READER APP

The Kindle reader app on Mac comes in handy for you if you purchase, borrow, or rent books from Amazon. By signing into your Amazon account, you can get access to all the Amazon books that are in your library. Please note that it is not possible for you to browse the Amazon books store from the Kindle app. However, the book will be added to your collection when you buy a book on Amazon.

This way, you will be able to access it from all your devices, whether they are Apple, Windows, or Android. Amazon supports the renting, borrowing, and sampling of books, among other services. Prime readers benefit more from Amazon because they get offered hundres of free eBooks and magazines.

There is a subscription-based service called Kindle Unlimited. This service offers a monthly price to read about a million titles. Kindle on Mac also has numerous customization features as well. It allows you to adjust the font size and style to suit your reading experience. In addition to that, you can also change the theme to sepia, white, or black. Kindle also allows you to add notes and highlights. One of its other outstanding features is to allow you to browse through popular highlights from other readers who have read the book.

ADOBE DIGITAL EDITIONS

Adobe Digital Editions (ADE) is an ePub reader that makes it easy to read digital books on your Mac. You do not have to upload them to a cloud server or drag them into an app.

Once you have ADE on your Mac, you can set it as the reader for any ePub file and you can commence reading instantly.

With ADE, you can highlight text, add a bookmark, and even add notes to passages and pages.

BOOK READER APP

The BookREader app supports all files, from EPUB, MOBI, RTF, PRC, AZW, FB2, Microsoft DOC, RTFd, TXT, xHTML, and Webarchive. Any type of eBook can be read on BookReader. Please note that BookReader only supports DRM-free files, so before you try to utilize it, ensure that your digital books do not have digital rights protection.

For easy access, store all your books on one shelf. The BookReader app has features to provide a pleasant reading experience on Mac. For example, there is realistic page-flipping, Text to speech, a fully customizable color option, and hypertext support.

OVERDRIVE READ

OverDrive allows you to borrow digital content from your local public library. What is needed is an active library card and a PIN. This app lets you check out multiple titles and browse your library's whole collection of digital content at the same time. When you borrow an item or an eBook, you will be able to download it on your Mac and have unlimited access to it during your loan period. However, there is no need to return the book to the library. Once your eBook is due, it will automatically be removed from your Mac. How convenient!

The OverDrive Read app on Mac is a software program that is supported by the web browser. Although it can be accessed from a web browser, it is possible for you to download content for offline use, be it watching, reading, or listening. Remember to bookmark the page so that you will be able to access it without an internet connection. In cases when you have remembered to download the content while online, it is possible for you to continue reading while offline.

Some of the features that OverDrive Read has include tools for adjusting the size and style of font, changing the font color, voice-over, highlighting, and adding notes. The app also supports fixed-layout digital books such as magazines and comics. This lets your favorite illustrated content not appear weird on your Mac.

Watching TV and Movies

You can buy, rent, and browse the world's best movies and TV shows on the store pane in the Apple TV app. When you find something that you want to watch, you can rent, purchase, or choose how you intend to watch it if it is available on multiple apps and channels. Suppose it is readily available, you will get the default application or channel that allows you to watch it in the highest possible quality.

BROWSING MOVIES AND TV SHOWS

On your Mac, **go to the Apple TV app, click Store** at the top of the window. **Afterward, click Movies or TV Shows**. After that, scroll to browse featured genres, collections, and items. As you scroll, recommendations will appear based on your tastes, past viewing, rental, or purchase history.

In any category, if you want to see more items, scroll right or left, or click See All. If you wish to return to the previous screen, click the Back button. For every item that you click, you will be able to see descriptions, ratings, viewing information, and previews.

PICKING A TV SHOW OR MOVIE TO WATCH

To pick a TV show or movie to watch on your Mac, **go to the Apple TV app, click Store** at the top of the Window. After that, **click Movies or TV shows.** When you click on an item, there are many available options to choose from.

For instance, you could play a movie or TV show. If the movie or TV show is available to you on a certain channel or as a purchase, you can click play so that you can start watching it instantly.

You could also buy or rent a movie by selecting Buy or Rent. Afterward, it is important to confirm your purchase or rental. Depending on your region, you can rent movies and be given 30 days to commence watching a rented movie. Suppose you have started watching the rented movie, you are free to play it as many times as you wish, within a period of 48 hours. It is possible for you to download the rented movie on one device and stream it on another, during the rental period. Once the rental period is over, the movie will no longer be available *(Apple, 2022e).*

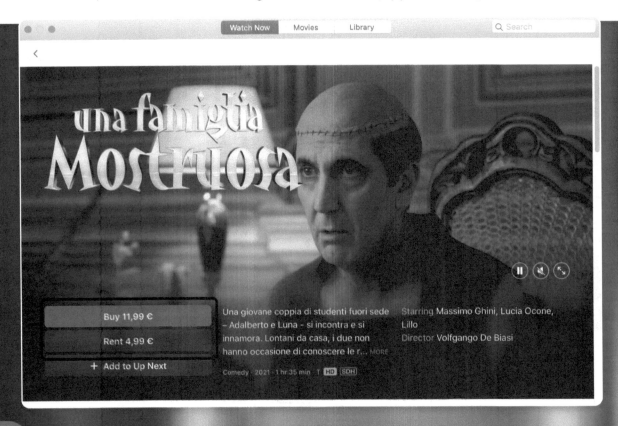

Another option at your disposal is to buy a season or an episode. To do so, click Buy, then select the option that you want prior to confirming your purchase. In case you have a TV show or movie that you want to watch later, you can add an item to Up Next. Click Add to Up Next so that you will add it to the Up Next row in Watch Now. To indicate that the item has been added, the Add to Up Next button changes to In Up Next.

If it so happens that you have changed your mind about watching the movie or TV show, go ahead and click In [1] [2] [3] Up Next. You can scroll down to access more information relating to browsing episodes and seasons, watching additional trailers, previewing extras, exploring cast and crew, viewing options, and browsing related items.

If you are using an Apple device, the iTunes Store is best when it comes to streaming and watching movies. Due to the fact that iTunes is Mac's very own app, it is extremely user-friendly. Besides, you can watch a whole host of rented or purchased movies. In case you don't have a Mac but would like to use the features of the iTunes Store, the good news is that you can also play these movies on Windows PC.

You could also stream your favorite movies on Mac using the Amazon Video on Demand *(Easy, 2021)*. The Amazon Video on Demand platform works perfectly on your MacBook through the use of a web browser. However, it is worth noting that some of its features are incompatible with the MacBook. As long as you know how to optimize the features for your system, Amazon Video on Demand is a brilliant way to watch movies.

Watch Videos with QuickTime or VLC

The first choice for Mac users is **QuickTime Player**. This is because it is bundled with Mac OS X. It is better **to choose VLC Media Player if you are a Windows user.** The major difference between the two players is that QuickTime Player can play iTunes M4V movies, whereas VLC Media Player cannot directly play M4V movies.

Non-Apple devices such as VLC Media Player cannot play iTunes M4V movies because the iTunes M4V movies have Digital Restriction

Management (DRM) protection, a technology that controls what you are able to do with the devices and digital media that you possess.

However, if you are interested in enjoying iTunes movies on VLC Media Player, you can download NoteBurner M4V Converter Plus, which is a powerful DRM removal tool. NoteBurner M4V Converter Plus is able to record iTunes purchases and rentals. Once you remove the iTunes DRM, you can convert movies to different formats such as AVI, MOV, and MP4 *(Noteburner-video, 2022)*.

Apple developed an extendable multimedia framework called QuickTime Player. You can get it for free when you are using OS X and Windows operating systems.

QuickTime Player handles various formats of digital video, sound, picture, interactivity, and panoramic images. One of the main features of the QuickTime Player is that it fully supports Mac OS X. Also, QuickTime Player is able to save existing QuickTime movies directly to a hard disk drive from the web.

QuickTime also encodes and transcodes audio and video from one format to the other. In addition to that, QuickTime is able to save the embedded video in a *.mov file format or its original format no matter what the origins are. Other video players that you can use to watch videos on your Mac include Wondershare Filmora, 4.5K Player, Cisdem VideoPlayer, MPlayerX, and Elmedia Player *(Mattison, 2022)*.

CHAPTER 7:
MAPS AND OTHER APPS

Apple designed numerous applications that came with the exceptional devices that they introduced. This chapter will focus on Maps and other applications that were put forward by Apple. You can do many things with the Maps apps, from getting directions to planning your route, all with a 3D view of iconic places. In addition to Maps, there are other remarkable apps as well. Let's get more details on Maps and other apps in this chapter.

Using Maps to Explore the World

It is possible for you to explore the world using the Maps app on Mac. The application allows you **to get directions for walking, cycling, taking public transportation, and driving**. For quick access on the go, you may as well **send directions to your Apple Watch, iPad, or iPhone.**

In the **Maps app** on your Mac, click the **Directions button in the toolbar**. Afterward, **enter your current location and destination**. Click your destination—for example, a pin on a map or a landmark—prior to clicking Directions in the place card. **Maps uses your current location as your starting point**. However, it is possible to enter a different one.

The Swap Directions button allows you to swap your starting and finishing points. Depending on your preferences, you can click the Walk, Drive, Bicycle, or Transit button *(Gil, 2016)*. To see the list of possible directions that you can take, click the Trip Details button.

In case you are driving, take note that directions can include electric vehicle routing, congestion zones, and license plate restrictions. If your vehicle is compatible, you can keep track of your current charge. You could also see charging stations that are along your way.

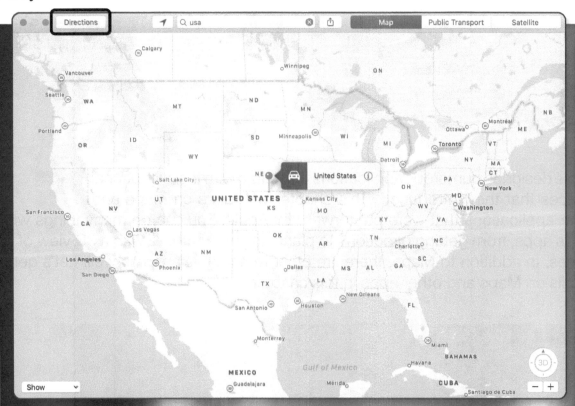

When you are in major cities such as Paris, Singapore, and London, the Maps app can give you a heads-up on congested zones. This helps reduce traffic in dense areas by providing you with routes around the congested zones. When it comes to license plate restrictions, there are some Chinese cities that limit access to dense areas. The Maps app can help you get around or through a restricted area based on how eligible you are.

Depending on which city you are in, directions can be provided if you are bicycling. For public transportation and driving, you can choose when to depart or arrive. Simply click Plan to choose when you want to leave or arrive. To close the directions list, click again on the Trip Details button.

SHOWING THE 3D MAP IN MAPS

By utilizing the 3D tool in the Maps app, you can get a more realistic view of a certain location. The application has a way of simulating building structures so that you can get a more detailed idea of how the area looks. Once you have enabled the 3D map, remember to zoom in close so that you can really see what it is capable of doing.

From the Dock or Finder, launch the **Maps app**. In the bottom left corner of the Maps window, click Show, **then Show 3D Map**.

From there, you can click and drag the 3D icon that you find at the bottom right corner of the screen. This helps you to decrease or increase your view of the 3D buildings. To rotate your view, click and drag the compass in a circular motion. The compass is at the bottom right corner of the screen.

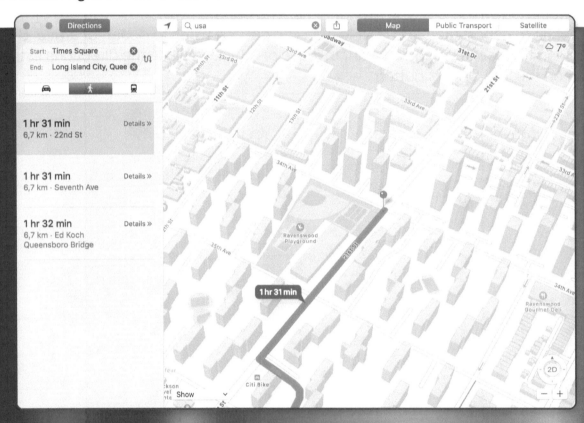

USING THE FLYOVER ON MAPS

The Maps development team at Apple has given special attention to some destination spots around the world. **Flyover is an exceptional feature that allows you to have a visual adventure across a city.** You will have an opportunity to fly around, thereby taking a look at iconic spots such as Buckingham Palace in London and the Eiffel Tower in Paris.

Go to your Dock or Finder to open the Maps app. Search for a **Flyover city**, then **enter a location**. Next to the 3D Flyover Tour tab at the bottom center of the screen, **click the Start option**.

Once you click on the Start option, you will be taken on a visual adventure across the city. Simply click on End when you are done enjoying and want to stop the tour *(Gil, 2016)*.

Enter a location

Flyover Tour

Planning a Route on Your Mac

It is crucial to plan a route on your Mac before a cycling day or a big trip. Simply ensure that you are signed in on your device and on your Mac with the same Apple ID. This will allow you to share the details with another device. To plan a route on your Mac, you should follow the next steps. On your Mac, go to the Maps app and click a location on the map, be it a landmark, business, or intersection.

In the place card, click Create Route before entering the destination in the To field. Another option would be to click the **Swap Directions button** ⟨↑↓⟩, prior to entering the starting point in the From field. If need be, you could also click Directions, then alter the starting and ending locations.

After that, click Plan. Select Leave or Arrive to choose when you want to leave your starting point or reach your destination, respectively. To enter a new date, you can select it from the calendar or click the date to enter a new one.

Time is of the essence when you want to plan a route. Therefore, you should also click the time you intend to leave or arrive. **If you are driving, it is possible for you to click Options, then Choose to avoid highways and tolls if you wish.**

In the case of taking public transportation, you can choose which transit options you desire to use, be it bus or ferry. **In the toolbar, click the Share button** ⟨↥⟩, **then choose the device that you wish to send directions to.** You will receive a notification on your device. To open directions in Maps, simply tap the notification.

Sending Directions to Your other Device

It is possible to send Directions to Your iPad, Apple Watch, or iPhone. If you are signed in with your Apple ID on both your Mac and your other device, you can send a location or directions to other devices. In the **Maps app** on your Mac, **click a location on the map.** Prior to making any adjustments that you would like to, **click Directions**.

Go to the toolbar and click the **Share button** ⟨↥⟩. **Select the device** that you want to send directions to. After these steps, **you will get a notification on your device.** To open the directions, **tap the Maps app on your device.**

Creating a Reminder

If you want to stay on top of your tasks, start using **Reminders on Mac**. With this application, **you are able to track your most important tasks** Keep your to-dos in sync on all your Apple devices through iCloud.

ADDING A REMINDERS ACCOUNT PROVIDER

From your Dock, open and click **Reminders** in the Menu bar. Afterward, click **Add Account** and choose the type you want—for example, iCloud. **Click continue and enter your account credentials. Click Sign In** and check the box that is next to Reminders.

Select the apps that your account should be used with. **Finally, click on Add Account.**

To create a reminder, go to your dock and open Reminders. Click the **+ button** and write out your reminder. If you want to schedule a due date for a reminder, click Reminders, then the Info button.

The Info option looks like an 'i' and it appears when you hover your cursor over the reminder. Click the On a Day option before entering the date for your reminder. After entering the date, also enter the time for your reminder, then click **Done.**

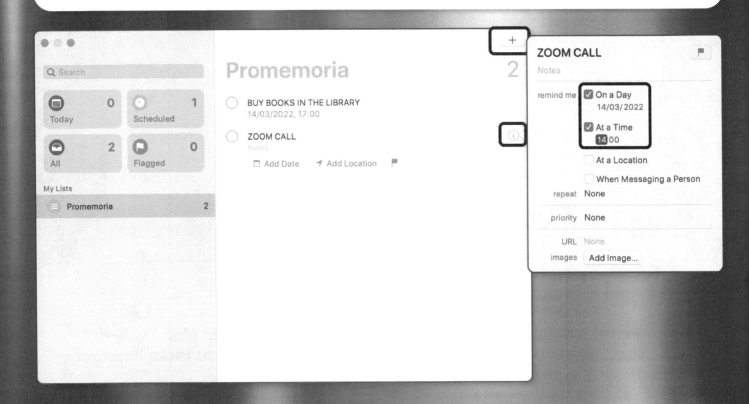

SETTING UP RECURRING REMINDERS

To set up a recurring reminder on your Mac, select the task that you want to set up the recurring reminder for. **Under Item Details, go to Reminders and select it.** Upon selecting the Reminders option, a small window will pop up.

On that small window, **select the Repeat option** and you will see a drop-down menu. **From the dropdown menu, choose the option you wish** to set for recurring reminders, then select it. Take note that you can choose to set your reminder on an hourly, daily, weekly, monthly, or yearly basis. When you follow these steps, your recurring reminders will be set *(appfluence.com, 2021).*

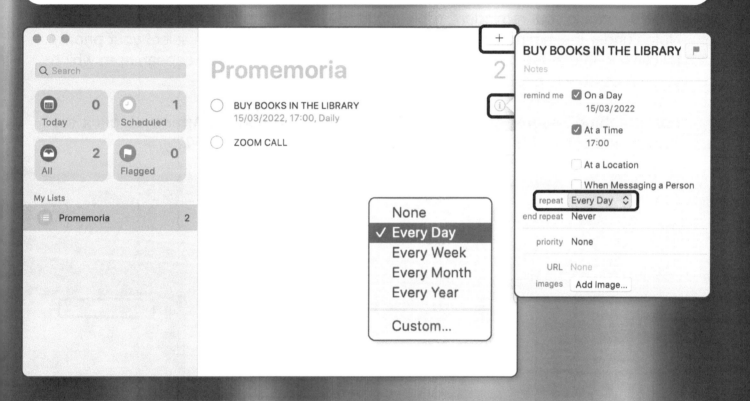

SETTING UP A LOCATION NOTIFICATION FOR A REMINDER

From your Dock, open Reminders and click Info. Click the box next to At a Location and enter a location for your reminder. You can choose either Leaving or Arriving, then drag the dot on the map closer or away from the pin to set the location in which your reminder should trigger. Click Done.

ATTACHING ITEMS TO REMINDERS

It is possible to add images, notes, URLs, as well as priority to reminders. This comes in handy for different types of reminders, especially if you utilize the app for school or work.

To add notes to your reminders, click Info at the right of the reminder. Afterward, click Notes under the reminder name, then type in your notes. You can select your priority by clicking Info at the right of the reminder. A drop-down box will appear, from which you will be able to choose the priority, be it low, medium, or high.

For attaching images, click Info at the right of the reminder. After that, click the Add Image option for you to attach the photo. *(Writtenhouse, 2020).*

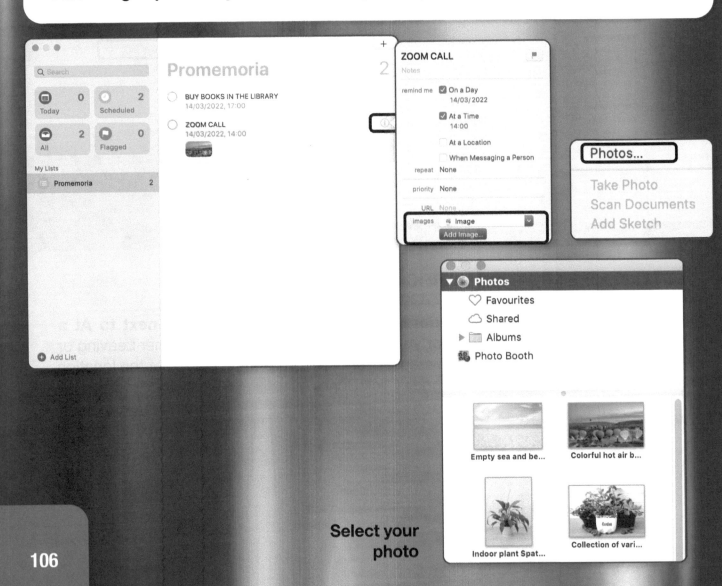

Select your
photo

CREATING, RENAMING, AND DELETING A LIST

To create a new list of reminders, open Reminders and click Add List. The next step is **to assign a name and enter it.** Should you want to rename the list, open Reminders and right-click on the list that you want to rename. Afterward, click Rename and enter the new name for your list.

To delete a list, open Reminders from your Dock and **right-click on the list** that you would like to delete. Finally, **click Delete** *(Keller, 2019).*

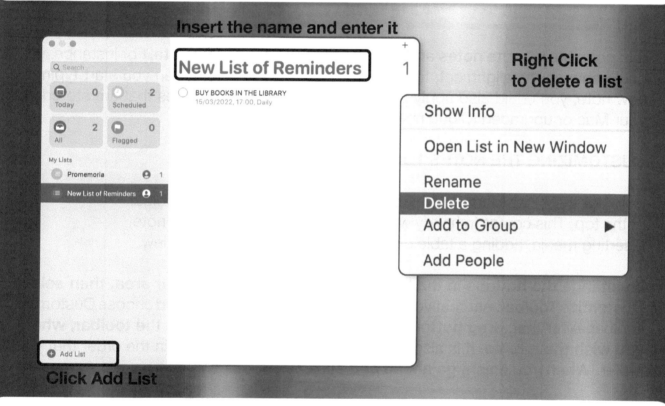

Insert the name and enter it

Right Click
to delete a list

Click Add List

MOVING A REMINDER TO A DIFFERENT LIST

To move a reminder to a different list, open Reminders from your Dock. After that, **click on the list** that contains the reminder that you want to move. On that list, click and hold the reminder that you want to move, then **drag the reminder** over the list that you intend to move it to.

SHARING A LIST WITH ANOTHER ICLOUD USER

To share a list with another iCloud user, go to your Dock and **open Reminders. Click the Share button** next to the list that you want to share. Afterward, **enter the contact** that you wish to share the list with, **then click Done.**

Creating, Modifying, and Sharing Notes

It is possible to write notes and change the formatting in a note. For instance, you could change the alignment, font size, or write in bold text. When you start typing a new note, you could also apply paragraph styles if you use notes that are stored on your Mac or upgraded iCloud notes.

CUSTOMIZING THE NOTES TOOLBAR

Just like the other Mac apps, Notes contains a customizable toolbar at the top. This comes in handy when it comes to creating a new note, inserting media, adding a table or checklist, and changing your view.

To change the buttons in the toolbar, right-click in the toolbar area, then select Customize Toolbar. Alternatively, from the menu bar, click View and choose Customize Toolbar. After that, **drag buttons from the bottom options into the toolbar, where you wish them to be.** It is also possible to arrange the buttons in the order that you prefer. **When you finish, go ahead and click Done.**

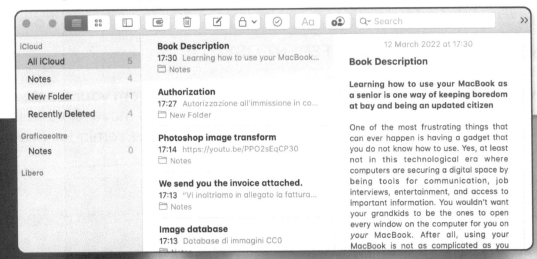

You will notice that a button or two may disappear from the toolbar. This is probably due to the window size. If the window is not wide enough to accommodate all the buttons that you choose, look for the arrow to the right of the Search box. Simply click that arrow to see your other buttons *(Writtenhouse, 2020)*.

WRITING A NEW NOTE

On your Mac, **go to the sidebar in the Notes app** and click the folder where you want to put the note. In case you do not see the sidebar, simply click View, then Show Folders.

Click the New Note option that you find in the toolbar and type your note. If available, you can use typing suggestions. The first line of the note serves as the note's title. You can possibly change the first line's formatting in Notes preferences. Please note that as you work, your note is automatically saved.

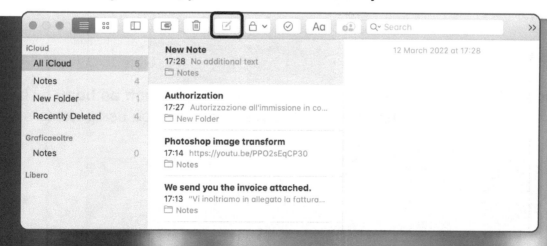

EDITING A NOTE

To edit a note on your Mac, go to the Notes app and click a note in the notes list. You could also double-click a note in the gallery view. To quickly find the Notes app, you could also search for notes. **In the note text, click where you want to edit** or select the text that you wish to alter, then make your alterations.

CREATING A COPY OF A NOTE

In the Notes app on your Mac, click an unlocked note. Afterward, **choose File, then Duplicate Note.** Alternatively, you could press **Command and D** on your keyboard.

COPYING AND PASTING TEXT

In the Notes app on your Mac, double-click a note in gallery view or click a note in the notes list. **To copy all the text in a note, start by selecting all the text. Click anywhere in the note text**, then **choose Edit** prior to clicking on **Select All**.

An alternative way of **highlighting all the text** is to use the keyboard shortcut of pressing **Command and A.** After highlighting all the text, **choose Edit, then Copy.** Alternatively, press **Command and C. To paste text, select Edit, then Paste**, or press **Command and V.** When you paste, some formatting is retained, while the original color and font may not be retained *(Apple, 2022q).*

To paste text using the surrounding style, select Edit, then Paste and Match Style. When you want to paste text using the original style, select Edit, then Paste and Retain Style. The copied text stays with the style information and when the text is pasted, it will have the original style applied. **You can also utilize Universal Clipboard to copy images, text, videos, and photos on one Apple device, then paste the items on another.**

FORMATTING TEXT

To quickly format a paragraph, you can apply a style such as body or heading. Take note that for you to use paragraph styles, you must be using notes stored on your Mac or upgraded iCloud notes. When formatting text on your Mac, go to the Notes app and double-click a note in gallery view or click a note in the notes list.

If you wish to change the formatting of selected text—for example, changing a phrase to bold—simply select the text and click the Format button Aa . Afterward, choose the desired option.

To change the text alignment, click anywhere you wish to change in the text. Choose Format in Menu Bar, then Text, prior to choosing the option that you want.

To change the text size, color, and font, select the text you wish to change. Control-click the selection, select Font, then Show Fonts. After that, make the changes using the Fonts window. If you want to apply a style to a paragraph, click anywhere in the text that you want to format. The next step is to click the Format button, then select a style.

To change the default title paragraph style, select Notes, then Preferences. You will see a pop-up menu from which you should click New notes to start with. Afterward, choose an option.

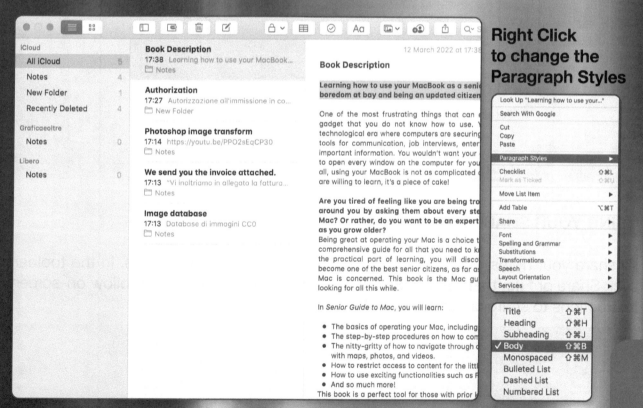

Right Click to change the Paragraph Styles

SHARING YOUR NOTES

You may want to share notes on different applications or with other people. This helps you to efficiently collaborate in a manner that works best for you. Suppose you have a specific note that you want another person to edit or view, follow the next steps.

From the toolbar, click Add People ⟨👥⟩ . Alternatively, from the menu bar, click File, then Add People To. Choose the name of your note.

From here, it is important to **choose the method you prefer** to share the note with that person, be it **Messages, AirDrop, or Mail**. Next to Permission, select either Only people you invite can view or Only people you invite can make changes. If applicable, complete the Add field, then click Share prior to following the prompts to invite a friend to look at your note *(Writtenhouse, 2020)*.

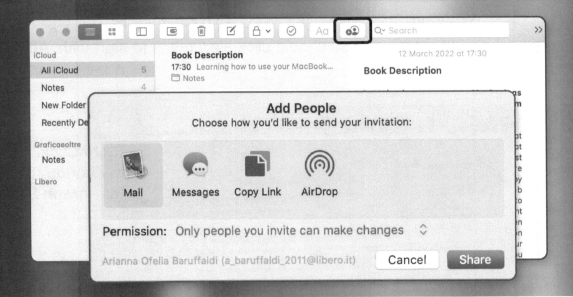

USING YOUR SHARE MENU

To share your notes, you could use the Mac Share Menu extensions. In the toolbar, click Share or **File, then Share**. Select the service or your app, then follow on-screen instructions to share or send your note.

NOTE-TAKING APPS FOR MAC

In addition to the Notes app, there are other note-taking apps that you can use on your Mac. These include Microsoft OneNote, Apple Notes, Obsidian, Bear, and Joplin. The advantages of these apps are that they efficiently add notes, are user-friendly, and help you in organizing your notes. Furthermore, these apps provide fast and useful searches *(Pot, 2021)*.

Using a MacBook to Pick a Call

Imagine a situation where your iPhone is ringing, you need to answer the call, but you are just too lazy to go and get it. **With a feature called iPhone Cellular calls, it is possible for you to answer that call using a nearby Mac or iPad.**

The feature is part of Apple's Continuity system, which is built to share and sync certain capabilities across iPadOS, iOS, Mac, and the Apple Watch. For you to use this feature, your iPad must have at least iOS 8 or iPadOS, while your iPhone must be running on iOS 8.1 or later and activated with a carrier. **The operating system for your Mac must be OS X Yosemite or later.** In case you have a Mac Pro or Mac Mini, it must also possess an external headset or microphone to utilize this feature.

As mentioned earlier, **each device must be signed in to FaceTime and iCloud with the same Apple ID**. In addition to that, **they must be Wi-Fi enabled and connected to the same network, be it Ethernet or Wi-Fi.**

ANSWERING OR DECLINING CALLS ON YOUR MAC

When a call notification appears in the top-right corner of the screen on your Mac, **you can accept an incoming call by clicking Accept** *(Whitney, 2022).* If the person that is calling you has set up Real Time Text (RTT) for the call and you prefer to answer it that way, click RTT.

If you want to decline a call, simply click Decline. In case the call has come from someone you are not comfortable receiving calls from, you can block the caller.

In some cases, you may not be able to answer a call but you can respond by sending a message to the caller. **To decline a call and respond by sending a message using iMessage, click next to Decline, prior to choosing**.

After that, type your message, then click send. You must both be signed in to iMessage for this communication to work. At times, you may want to decline a call and set a reminder to call back later. In this case, click next to Decline and select the amount of time you prefer to wait before you receive a reminder. You will get a notification when the time comes. Simply click it to view the reminder. Afterward, click the link in the reminder so that you can start the call.

If your Mac has a Touch Bar, you can easily use it to accept, decline, decline and set a reminder, or decline and send a message.

CHAPTER 8:

SYSTEM PREFERENCES

Your Mac has a lot of settings and preferences that are meant to control the functions and effective use of the device. All these settings are well organized in one app, which is known as system preferences.

To access System preferences, go to the Apple Menu . The variety of options that are available in System preferences makes it possible for you to customize your Mac to what appeals to you. In this chapter, we will look at various ways through which you can use System preference.

System Preferences App

When you open System Preferences, you will discover many icons that represent different things that you can play around with to customize your Mac. Each of the **icons that you see in System Preferences represents something different. You can** regard the icons as the windows to different settings and options.

Generally, System Preferences has three, sometimes four sections. At the top of the window, you will find your name. On your right, there are two icons. These icons will direct you to Family Sharing and Apple ID.

Toward the lower side of the screen, you will find icons that are categorized into two sections. One section focuses on personal settings, while the other set of icons is responsible for customizing how your Mac interacts with hardware.

The fourth section is made up of third-party apps that you install onto your Mac. For instance, you can backup your data using Backblaze, a third-party app that installs a preference pane. The latter assists with configuring the features of the Backblaze app.

Therefore, if there is nothing that is installed in your Mac, your System Preferences will have three sections. The icon arrangement that we just described can be quite confusing, considering that there is no precise order. It is even difficult to find some of the icons when you need them.

It is possible to rearrange the icons in alphabetical order, irrespective of the categories to which they belong. Such an arrangement will help you to locate icons with enhanced ease. **To change the arrangement of icons in System Preferences, select View and then click Organize Alphabetically.** They will rearrange themselves accordingly.

Suppose, you don't want to change the way icons are displayed in the Systems Preference app, yet you don't want to struggle with locating them. You can access the various icons via the grid button. Located in the toolbar, the grid button also displays icons in their alphabetical order. Besides, you can even see the whole menu for System Preferences when you click the View menu.

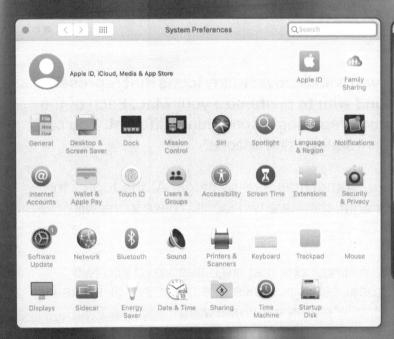

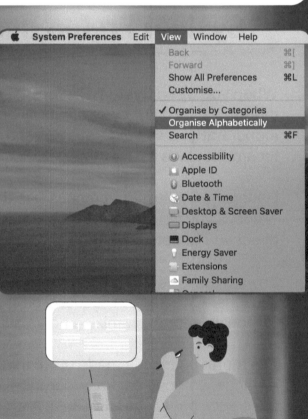

Hiding Icons

Since there are other alternatives to accessing the icons that are in System Preferences, the frequency at which you might visit this app differs with individuals. You might visit it on a regular basis or once in a while. If you are one of those people who use the System Preferences app more frequently, then you need some tips on how to make navigating through the app as easier as it can be.

One of the things that you can do is hide the apps that you are not currently using or those that you might never use at all. This way, fewer icons that are relevant to what you do with your device are left and are easier to manage. Navigating through them is also less time-consuming.

To hide some icons in the System Preferences app, select View, before clicking Customize. When you do this, all the icons will show on the screen, alongside checkmarks close to each of them. **Go on and uncheck all the icons that you don't necessarily need.**

For instance, uncheck Siri if you don't use it. Again, there is no point in keeping the Startup Disk when you only have one drive that is connected to your device. You can, therefore, uncheck the Startup Disk.

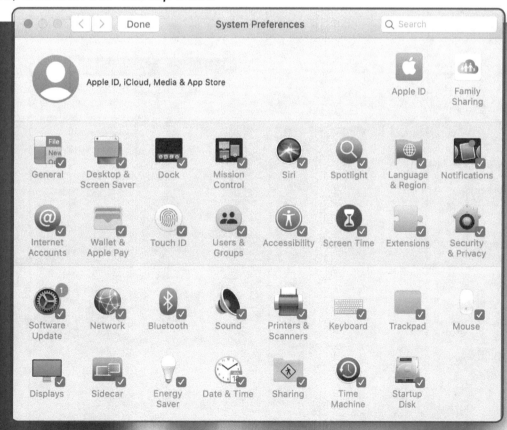

Using the Search Function

Finding settings is also easy when you use the search option in System Preferences. There are some settings that you can easily find because there are fewer options under a certain icon.

For example, the Software update panel is quite easy to navigate through, with only one checkbox. It also has an Advanced options button that allows you to alter some settings as relevant or to your preference. The challenge of finding the settings that you want is evident when you open panes such as the Security and Privacy one.

There are too many options under this pane, so getting what you want might be difficult. This is where the search functionality comes into play.

The next question would be, **"How then do you know the search words to use as you look for certain settings in System Preferences?"** This is quite simple.

Suppose the setting that you're looking for is the one that makes it possible for certain apps to access some files on your Mac, you might have the idea of the pane that contains such settings the Security and Privacy panel *(McElhearn, 2020)*.

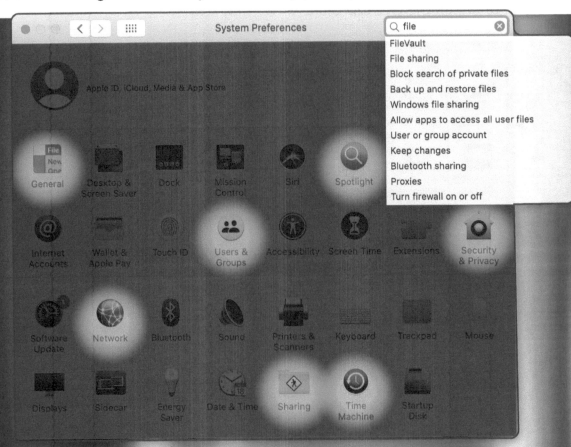

Let's say you have no idea which section of the Security and Privacy pane has the setting, you can type the word 'file' in the search box available. The app will give you many options so that you can choose the best possible one among them.

The suggestion that you choose will take you to the settings that you are looking for. If not, just play around with the keywords that relate to the setting that you are searching for. Once you get to the settings that you want, follow the prompts.

Monitor Settings

You can customize monitor settings on your MacBook. This contributes to creating an environment that you enjoy or, rather, that suits you. For instance, it is possible to alter settings such as brightness to match your preferences. If you have problems with your eyesight, you should avoid looking at too bright screens, especially for extended periods of time. In this section, the main focus is on giving you ideas on how you can adjust monitor settings. Let's dive in!

ADJUSTING BRIGHTNESS

Adjusting the brightness on your Mac begins by **clicking on the Apple menu** . This menu is available on the top left corner of your screen. **Go to System Preferences** and **select Displays**. In some cases, you will find a slider that you can move to and forth to adjust the brightness on the screen of your Mac.

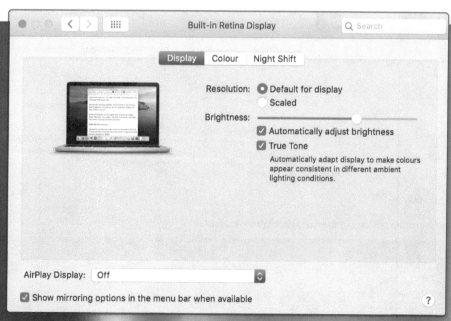

Sometimes, you simply have to check or uncheck on Automatically adjust brightness, depending on what is best for you. For example, if you're comfortable with the device-determined brightness settings that your computer will set for you, check Automatically adjust brightness. Special brightness requirements are best met when you do the adjustments manually.

Changing Resolution

Altering the resolution on your MacBook is not as complicated as you might think. **Go to the Apple menu** , **click System Preferences**, and then **select Displays**.

In the event that the Resolution is set to Default with regard to display, click Scaled. To the left of Default, there are boxes that you can click on if you want to enlarge the text. Would you prefer more space on the screen so as to accommodate many things? If yes, simply click one of the boxes that are located at the right of Default.

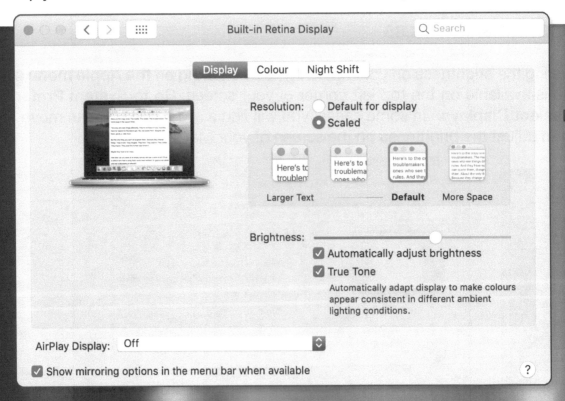

Altering Reference Modes

Reference modes help to set characteristics of various media types, including SD, HD, and HDR videos. They set the white space, brightness, color space, and gamma on the display of the media types. As such, you can alter the reference modes to match your preferences.

If you want to adjust the reference modes, open the Apple Menu, go to System Preferences, and then choose Displays. A Presets pop-up menu will appear, click it to select the reference mode that you want to adjust. An alternative method for adjusting reference modes is by going to the Menu bar and then **clicking on the Airplay menu. Click Reference Modes.** Now you know how to adjust reference modes, but do you know how to choose the ones that are dear to you? To choose a reference mode, go to the Apple menu, System Preferences, and then Displays. Click the Presets menu that pops up prior to choosing Customize Presets. Different reference modes will appear, select the ones that you want, and then click Done.

Interestingly, **you can also create custom reference modes**. This is an advanced option that allows custom reference modes to be weaved in ways that produce enhanced workflows that are unique in nature. This involves creating your preferred combinations of, say, the luminance, color gamut, transfer function, and white point functions.

To get this done, open the Apple menu, then System Preferences, and finally, Displays. After **clicking on the Presets pop-up menu and the Customize Presets**, one after the other, **select the + icon** that is located at the bottom left side of your screen. **You can then select a Preset name**, prior to making the adjustments that you want. **Click Save the Preset and you are good to go**!

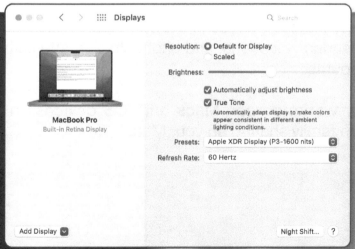
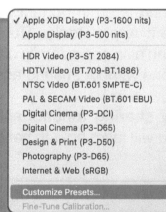

Displays

Adjusting the Refresh Rate

Some versions of Mac, like the MacBook Pro (2021), have the functionality that allows you to change the refresh rate. Some of the refresh rates that are available are 47.95 Hertz, 48 Hertz, 50 Hertz, 59.94 Hertz, and 60 Hertz. The moment you make the decision to change the refresh rates, here is the number one tip: select the refresh rate that can be evenly divided into your content's frame rates. This means that the refresh rate that you will choose is highly dependent on the frame rate of your content. For instance, if your content's frame rate is 25 frames per second, the 50 Hertz refresh rate might be appropriate.

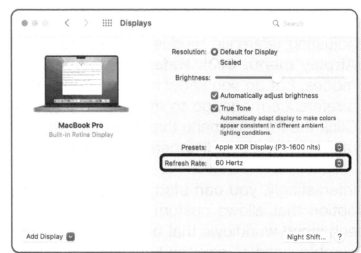

To start adjusting the refresh rate, open Displays by choosing the Apple menu and then System Preferences in their order of mention. When the Refresh Rates pop-up menu appears, click on it.

Select the refresh rate that you want and make sure it is appropriate with regard to the frame rate of your content.

Family Sharing

Family sharing is an important tool that allows a maximum of six people to share content, be it Apple Books, iTunes, Fitness+ subscriptions, or Apple Music Apple Plan. You can also share family calendars, locations, and photo albums. Interestingly, all this is done without sharing accounts.

The Family sharing functionality works across Macs and iOS devices. In this section, you will learn how to set up family sharing on your Mac.

SETTING-UP FAMILY SHARING ON MAC

The first step is to **open System Preferences**. This could be through your Dock or the Apple menu. **Click on Family Sharing,** which you will find at the top right side of the System Preference window. You will be required to confirm your Apple ID. After that, you will get prompts for inviting family members.

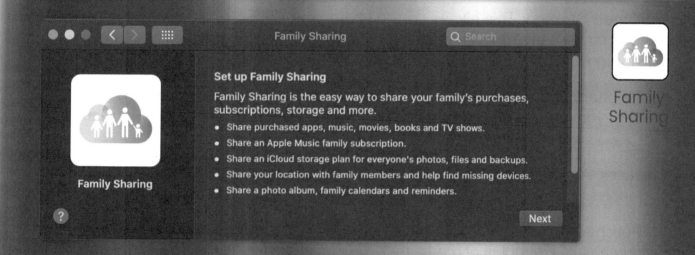

ADDING FAMILY MEMBERS

It is not mandatory that you add all the members of your family the moment you set up Family Sharing. It is possible to add them as you go and as you deem fit. You can even remove members if you choose to. Please note that you can only add up to a maximum of five family members.

Adding people to Family Sharing on a Mac involves **going to System Preferences prior to clicking Family Sharing**. Don't forget to select Family in the sidebar that is on the left side of your screen. **Click Add Family Member and you're done.** Each family member that you add to Family Sharing will receive an iMessage that serves as an invite to the Family.

The invited family members have the leverage to accept or deny being part of Family sharing. They have to tap on the iMessage and agree to join. Only then will Family Sharing work for them.

SELECTING FEATURES TO SHARE

Considering that there are many things that can be shared through Family Sharing, it is less likely that you want to share all of them. For this reason, you should select the features that are going to be shared with your family members. Here are some of the options that are available:

- **iCloud Storage:** This allows you to share your iCloud storage with members of your family. Let's say you have a storage plan that allocates you two terabytes of storage space, you can share this with your family members.

- **TV channels:** Suppose you subscribe to a Premium streaming service like Apple TV+, you can let your family also enjoy it without having to pay anything extra.

- **Screen Time:** Monitoring the screen time of a child in the family can become much easier. All you have to do is create a Child Account, set screen limits, and also view reports.

- **Purchase Sharing:** You can share any other media that you buy, except for in-app purchases. Examples of media that you can share include Books and iTunes.

- **Apple arcade**: You can even share Apple's gaming subscription service with the members of your family. They won't have to pay anything for them to access the service.

- **Location sharing:** It is possible for you and your family members to share your locations or those of your devices. However, please note this functionality is only available for people in the Find My app, which is a tool that helps to find the location of your device.

Having discussed some of the options that you may consider as you share features with your family, there are a few things that we need to clarify. These relate to some of the features that you may possibly share.

- **iCloud:** Some might fear that if they share iCloud storage with their family members, their data is exposed. This is not the case. People sharing an iCloud storage cannot see the information that is stored by other people they are sharing their storage space with. You only share the amount of data in numbers, but your storage spaces are completely separate.

- **Purchase sharing:** The moment you enable purchase sharing, the members of your family will access iTunes features, Books, and most of the apps that you purchase at the App Store. However, they will not access app subscriptions and in-app purchases. The moment you enable Purchase Sharing, anything involving purchases is charged to the Organizer of your family. This still applies even if the family member buys features that cannot be sharedthe Organizer still has to pay

- **Apple TV and Apple Music Channels:** When you share these channels, your content and playlists still remain private to yourself. In the same way, you cannot see the playlists of other family members too. When each of you access Apple Music or Apple TV, each of you has their separate recommendations and play history, just as it would be if they were paying their subscriptions on their own.

Restrict Content

It's good that gadgets like the Mac make it easy for kids to access information that is relevant to them. Such important information includes content that is related to their academic learning objectives. However, the internet can be a very unsafe environment for your grandkids if they access content that is toxic to them, like pornography.

Thank goodness Mac has functionalities that help you protect the hidden in your family from such harm. You can restrict content that can be streamed on a minor's account. The goal of this section is to discuss how you can restrict content on a MacBook.

CREATING A NEW USER ACCOUNT ON MAC

Usually, people have only one user account on Mac, which is also known as the administrator's account. If that is the case with you, then you should create another account for the minor in your home. For most seniors, this could be a grandchild or probably the youngest child.

To create this separate account for the child, **go to System Preferences** through your Dock. Among the options you see, **select Users and Groups.**

At the bottom left side of the screen, **you will see a lock, be sure to tap on it**. The next step would be to unlock your accounts and this requires you **to enter the username and password** of the administrator's account. Go to the bottom left side of the screen and **tap on the + that is there.**

Switch the type of account, putting forward Standard as your choice. You will then be required to enter the full name of the child you are opening the account for. Also, **create a password for that account** and verify it in response to prompts on your screen.

Creating a password hint is a great idea, just in case you forget it. **As the last step, click Create User and a new account will be created.** If there are more children staying with you, use the same procedure to create their own accounts too.

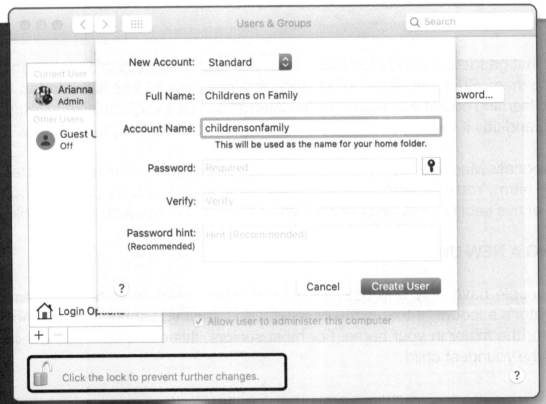

Turning on Screen Time on macOS

Now that the kids have their accounts, you don't want them to spend all their time staring at the screens. You can activate settings that give the kids restrictions as far as screen time is concerned. The first step in achieving that is turning onthe screen time. If you have never done it before, you are at the right place. This section will inform you on how to do it.

Open System Preferences and click Screen Time. Normally, the administrator account is selected by default. However, just check to make sure that it is selected. **Go to the Options button** that is located at the bottom left screen region and click it. At the top right side, **click Turn On.**

SETTING RESTRICTIONS ON ALL DEVICES

Screen Time has another function that allows you to put in place restrictions for all the devices in your home that children use. So, you set restrictions on one device, and the other devices pick up the same restriction. However, this does not just happen the devices should be set to do so. Let's delve into the nitty-gritty of how you can set your devices accordingly.

Through System Preferences, go to Screen Time. Again, just check if the administrator account is selected, it should always be by default. **Click the Options button** prior to checking the box that is adjacent to **Share across devices.** You're all set!

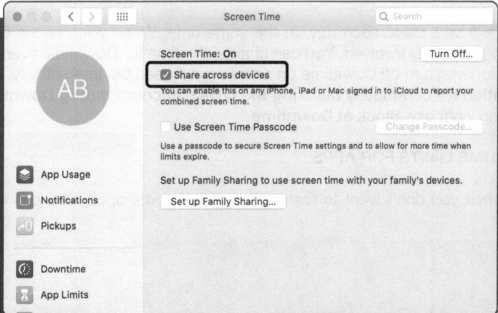

ADDING A PASSCODE TO SCREEN TIME

Advances in technology have gone to stages where children can easily navigate through devices and even customize settings to their own preferences. You wouldn't want that to happen in Screen Time because then the children can alter the restrictions that you would have put for them. You, therefore, need to add a passcode in a bid to avoid such a scenario.

Adding a passcode begins by selecting Screen Time, having entered System Preferences. Toggle the child's account and then click Options. Identify the Use Screen Time Passcode box and check it. **Enter a passcode with four digits** and then re-enter it as the prompts on the screen direct you.

USING SCREEN TIME FOR DOWNTIME SCHEDULING

Downtime refers to that moment where the other apps do not work on the child's account, except for the ones that you choose to allow. This comes in handy if there are certain apps that you want the child to focus on. They will have no option to use the apps that are working in their account at that given time. Downtime also works when there are some apps that are not bad for your child or grandchild, but you want to control the amount of time that the child spends on them.

To schedule Downtime for macOS, click System Preferences and then Screen Time. Toggle the child's account and then click Downtime. You will have to activate Downtime by clicking the **Turn-on button.** Decide on the schedule that you would like to set and then choose Custom or Every Day. When you select Every Day,

Downtime will take place each day, at the same time. When you choose Custom, there is more flexibility involved. You can change the time for Downtime every other day. You can even turn off Downtime on some days if need be. Interestingly, **there is also an option for completely blocking the child's account during Downtime.** To do this, simply **choose Block at Downtime.**

SETTING TIME LIMITS FOR APPS

At times when you don't want to restrict the use of some apps, you can limit the amount of time your child uses them. So in this case, you want the child to use the apps, but not for too long. Screen Time also has such functionalities.

To start, **open Screen Time in System Preferences. After toggling the child's account, click on App Limits.** You will find the latter on the left side of the screen.

Activate the time limits by clicking Turn on. Now, it's time to add the app category. Do so by clicking on the + symbol. Next to each app category is a check box. Check the one that is adjacent to the app category that you want to limit. Click on the Expand icon so that you can see the apps that are being affected by your selection. Highlight the app category before setting the time limit to your preference. Select either the Every Day or Custom schedule to determine the recurrence of the time limits.

 If there are other app categories that you would like to limit, follow the same procedure as described in this section. When all app categories of choice have been given time limits, click Done.

In the event that you then want to remove the time limits that you set, go back to Screen Time and toggle the child's account. Click on App Limits and then **uncheck each of the app categories whose time limits you want to drop.**

Click Turn Off in the event that you want to stop app tracking.

SETTING ALWAYS ALLOWED CONTENT

Depending on your assessment, there might be other content that you never look forward to restricting from the children. Such content is what we are referring to as "always allowed." **To set this up, open Screen Time, toggle the child's account,** and then **click on Always Allowed**. Go on and **check the boxes** that are adjacent to the time that **you want the child to always access without limitation.**

Security

Your Mac has security features that protect what is on your computer. During startup, the security features also stop unauthorized software applications from loading. **The Mac possesses secure storage, such that its drive is encrypted with keys that are tied to its hardware to provide extreme security.** However, if there is a catastrophic failure, it may be impossible to recover your data. Therefore, **it is important to back up your files on an external source.**

To back up your files on a regular basis, you can set up Time Machine on your computer or any other backup plan. Another security feature that you find on your Mac is the Secure boot and Startup Security Utility. The support for Secure boot is turned on automatically. It verifies that Apple authorizes the operating system software that is loaded on your computer at startup.

Your Mac will startup from a secure recovery partition and if possible, will automatically correct issues in the event that the computer has detected an untrusted component. In addition to that, your Mac has System integrity. **The MacBook Pro with Apple** silicon also verifies that the macOS software version loaded when starting up is **authorized by Apple.**

Furthermore, System integrity continues running behind the scenes to safeguard established authorizations for macOS. This makes it difficult for malicious websites and malware to invade your Mac.

Another security feature that you find on your Mac is Data Protection. In addition to the default storage drive encryption, third-party app developers are capable of using file-level encryption to improve the protection of sensitive data. This security feature is remarkable in that it does not impact the system's performance. **Please note that on rare occasions, such as a power failure during a macOS upgrade, your Mac may become unresponsive and the firmware on the chip might need to be repaired.** (Apple, 2022o).

Accessibility

The Accessibility Options panel provides shortcuts that help to quickly turn on or off common features such as Sticky Keys, Voice-Over, and Zoom.

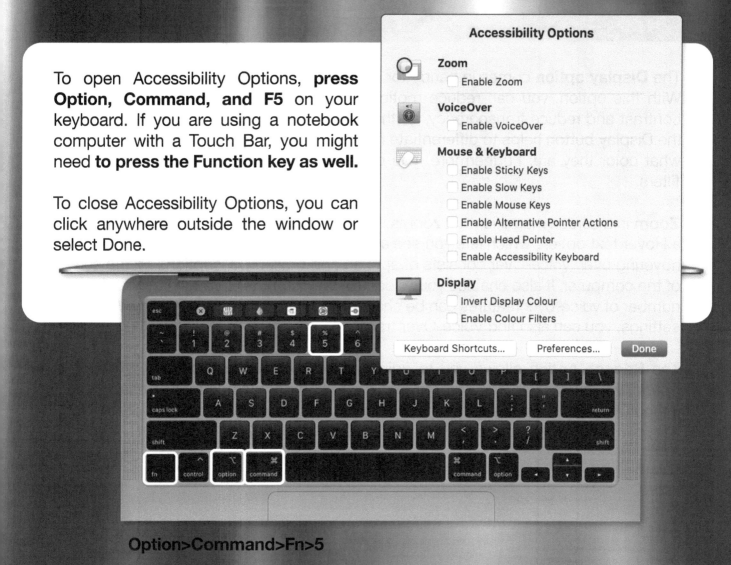

To open Accessibility Options, **press Option, Command, and F5** on your keyboard. If you are using a notebook computer with a Touch Bar, you might need **to press the Function key as well.**

To close Accessibility Options, you can click anywhere outside the window or select Done.

Option>Command>Fn>5

CHANGING THE SHORTCUTS IN ACCESSIBILITY OPTIONS

If you wish to change the shortcuts that appear in Accessibility Options, **go to the Apple menu and select System Preferences**. After that, **click Accessibility**. In the sidebar, **choose Shortcut, then use the checkboxes** to turn shortcuts off or on *(Apple, 2020)*.

Included in the Accessibility options are Display, Zoom, Voice-Over, Speech, and Captions.

The **Display option** comes in handy for people who experience visual disturbances. With this option, you can reduce motion and invert colors. You can also increase contrast and reduce transparency, so that items stand out more. In addition to that, the Display button helps to differentiate between options without needing to know what color they are. Furthermore, you can also change the contrast and set color filters.

Zoom is a screen magnifier that zooms in on the screen's smaller areas. There is also a Hover text option, which lets you see an enlarged form of the text that the mouse is hovering over. Voice-Over consists of spoken and broiled descriptions on the screen of the computer. It also enables you to control the computer through keyboard use. A number of voice-over features can be changed using the Voice-Over Utility. Within the settings, you can also find Voice-Over training.

The **Speech option** allows you to adjust computer settings for speech. With this option, you can set the computer to read the text under the pointer and enable visual announcements. Another option that you find under Accessibility is Captions, which allows you to adjust subtitle settings *(Kirklees Council, 2021)*.

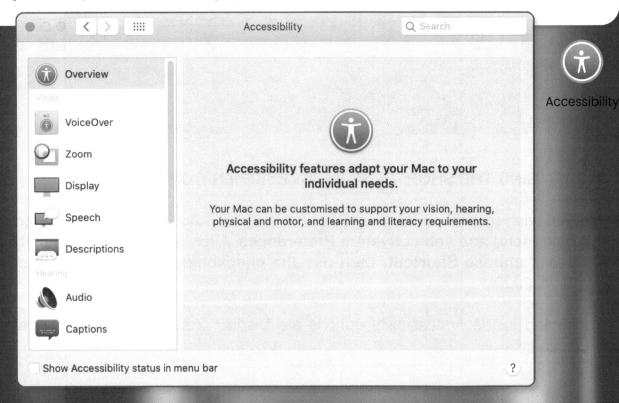

Accessibility

MacOS Updates

Newly discovered security gaps are quickly closed by Apple using security updates or complete "point updates" for the systems. It is important to note that these updates hardly cause problems. Therefore, keeping your system updated is essential. When Apple releases an update, it is usually incorporated with release notes that a security gap has been closed. With this, everyone will know that the previous version had a security gap. Sometimes, old systems and devices can no longer load the latest updates. The only answer in such a scenario is to make a new purchase *(Haslam, 2021).*

To update macOS on your Mac, go to the Apple menu in the corner of your screen and select System Preferences. Go ahead and **click Software Update** in the System Preferences window. Take note that if your System Preferences does not include Software Update, you may utilize the App Store to get updates instead. After clicking Software Update, **select Upgrade Now or Update Now**.

Update Now installs the most recent updates for the currently installed version, such as an update from macOS Monterey12.0 to the 12.3 one. When Software Update informs you that your Mac is up to date, it means that the macOS and all the apps are updated. These include apps such as Mail, Messages, Safari, Photos, Music, Calendar, and FaceTime. For downloaded apps, you may use the App Store to get their updates *(Apple, 2021d).*

CHAPTER 9: PRODUCTIVITY

After reading this chapter, you will be able to install VLC Media Player with a dmg file. A step-by-step guide on how you can install an application from the App Store is offered in this chapter. We will also discuss whether an Antivirus is useful or not. Let's get more information on the various ways to be productive on your Mac.

Installing VLC With DMG File

You will find the **VLC Media Player** on a number of platforms. This exceptional player is free and can be easily downloaded by Apple users. Generally, a dmg file is a physical disk that has been digitally reconstructed. Instead of using a physical disc, a dmg is a file format that is important for storing compressed software installers.

These file formats are mostly found on the internet in cases where macOS software downloads have to be completed. The macOS disk image format is good for encryption, file spanning, and compression *(Fisher, 2021)*.

OPENING A DMG FILE ON MAC

Due to the fact that dmg files are meant for Macs, opening them on these Apple devices presents itself as an easy task. **The operating system treats a dmg file like a physical hard drive.** As such, it becomes very easy when it comes to viewing its contents. Simply put, the dmg format software that you download on your Mac can easily be opened, just like the other files. In addition to that, you can run the setup program with ease in order to complete software installation.

To install VLC, you can download a dmg file by visiting http://www.videolan.org/ vlc/download-macosx.html. From here, you will see various download links, from which you will choose one depending on your operating system.

Also available on the above-mentioned site are two download links for web browser plugins. These links allow you to stream or play videos directly from your browser. After downloading the VLC installation file from the above-mentioned site, look for the downloaded file. It will be assigned a name such as vlc-2.1.0.dmg.

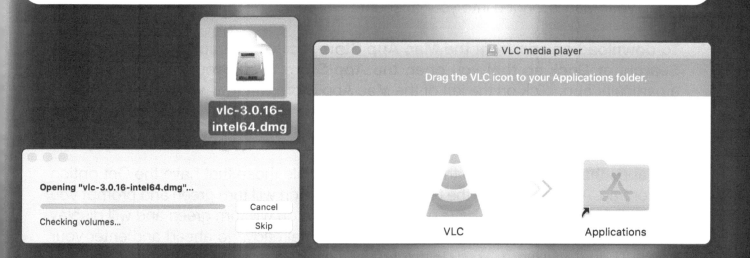

Open the downloaded file before clicking and dragging the VLC icon to the folder where applications are *(VLChelp, 2013)*. When you reach the applications folder, release it so that it will be copied there. Before providing permissions, the next step is to double-click the media player. Afterward, the VLC Media Player will be installed, and you can easily use it to play your media.

Downloading an App From the App Store

It is easy to download apps from the Mac App store. It is safe and requires the same login as the iPhone, iPad App Store, and iTunes. In relation to being safe, the apps found in the App Store are not only signed by their developers, but are reviewed by Apple's reviewers as well. Furthermore, re-downloading and updating apps is simple when your Mac is logged into your account.

To download an app from the Mac App Store, go to the Launch Pad, Spotlight Search, or Dock so that you open the App Store. When you want to download a particular app, click on the left of the Mac App Store window, where you will find various app categories as well as featured ones. Afterward, you can click on the price or the Get option to download the app *(Symons, 2020)*.

The apps that have prices on them are for sale, while those that have the Get option are for free. After clicking on the Get button, the option will turn green and prompt you to install. For the apps that have price tags, the button will turn green and will display the Buy App option. In case you are not signed in already, go ahead and enter your Apple ID and password. Your download will commence. Once it is complete, it will automatically go to the Finder in the Applications folder. You will be able to see your new App in the Launchpad app as well.

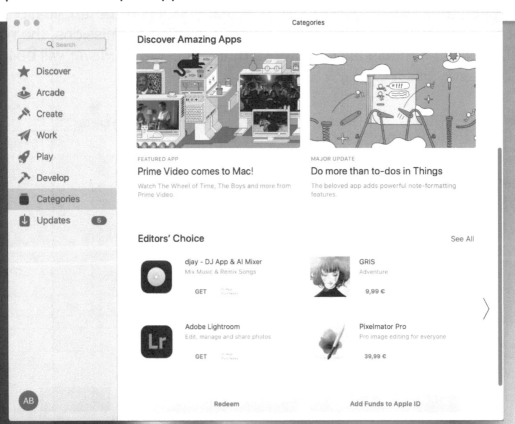

INSTALLING APPS PURCHASED ON A DIFFERENT DEVICE

Please note that you cannot make App Store purchase transfers from your Apple ID to another. **However, it is possible to install an app that you bought with your Apple ID to another device.** On your Mac, **go to the App Store** and **click your name in the bottom-left corner.** In case you are not already signed in, click the Sign In option. Find the purchased app that you wish to download. Afterward, **click on Download.**

AUTOMATICALLY DOWNLOADING PRE-PURCHASED APPS ON A DIFFERENT DEVICE

Go to the **App store on your Mac,** prior **to clicking your name** that is located on the bottom-left corner. **Ensure that you are signed in. Select the App Store**, then go to **Preferences**. Afterward, choose the option that says, **"Automatically download apps purchased on other devices"** *(Apple, 2022h).*

RE-INSTALLING APPS

You can delete or uninstall an App that you previously bought with your Apple ID, be it intentionally or unintentionally. The good news is that you can re-install the app if you wish. Prior to clicking your name in the bottom left, **go to the App Store on your Mac. Make sure that you are signed in.** Find the previously purchased app that you wish to reinstall. The next step is to **click the Download option and you are done.**

The Importance of an Antivirus

Although it is true that Mac computers are more secure than Windows systems, these Apple devices must have added protection through the use of antiviruses. The vulnerability of Macs to viruses and other malware is a quickly developing problem. In 2021, a study revealed that in 2020 alone there has been a 1000 percent increase in the level of malicious programs that target Mac computers *(Munson, 2022).*

In addition to the built-in security system of Apple devices that remarkably keeps malware at bay, you need to tighten your protection by installing antivirus software.

There are plenty of options when it comes to installing antivirus software on your Mac. Some of the ones that you can install include Norton, Intego, AVG, Kaspersky, and Bitdefender. Let's get more information on each of these antivirus software.

NORTON

To find the Norton virus software, visit www.Norton.com. This option is one of the best on the market. Norton has a 360 Deluxe AV tool. With this software, you qualified to be offered a first-year discount. The software has been reduced from a price of $104.99 and currently costs $39.99. Included in the Norton package are services that include VPN coverage, parental controls, and PC cloud backup. Furthermore, you can use it on five devices.

INTEGO

The antivirus software called Intego Mac Internet Security X9 is a friendly solution on the wallet. Its yearly price has been reduced from $84.99 to $39.99. This software was particularly built for Macs. In addition to other features that it offers, it possesses a location-based firewall and provides protection from phishing scams. You will find Intego on www.intego.com.

AVG

For simple virus protection, you can choose AVG's free tier. It allows you to scan for infected files on your Mac. The free tier also ensures that your new downloads are free of the virus payload. There is also an upgrade to the free tier. The paid AVG tier includes phishing and ransomware protection. In addition to that, it has a Wi-Fi inspector, which functions to monitor all the devices that are connected to your home network.

KASPERSKY

To find Kaspersky Internet Security for Mac, visit www. Kaspersky.com. Kaspersky usually has good scores in independent tests. From a price of $79.99, this software's price has been reduced to $39.99 for an entire year's protection. Kaspersky has webcam spying protection and a content filter that is used for parental control.

BITDEFENDER

Visit www.Bitdefender.com to access the Bitdefender Antivirus for Mac. This inexpensive option of protection has a number of features. It costs $29.99 for a whole year of protection from malware. Bitdefender Antivirus for Mac has an autopilot feature, in addition to a built-in Virtual Private Network (Munson, 2022).

Apple Suite iWork

With iWork, you can create exceptional word-processing documents, presentations, and spreadsheets. **The iWork office productivity suite has three apps, which include Pages, Numbers, and Keynote**.

These applications are free to anyone who possesses an Apple ID. Pages is a word processor app, whereas Numbers is an app for spreadsheets. The application for slideshows is Keynote.

In comparison to Google Docs and Microsoft Office, the iWork suite presents itself as a simple and easy-to-use alternative to the industry. iWork has a classy and clean design which makes it interesting to use. Although the iWork toolbar is simpler and cleaner, it actually has a more detailed toolset. The Format sidebar that is located on the right contains additional tools that help to beautify your work.

iWork has the advantage of storing your work in your iCloud account. This allows the instant syncing of work across all your Apple devices. Apple is exceptional. Its Handoff app allows you to continue with your work if you need to shift from your iPad to Mac. The iPad version has an added capability called the Apple Pencil. By using this Pencil, you can chart animation paths, shade, write short notes, and make drawings in your documents.

Pages

Pages, in Apple's words, can be described as "a canvas for creativity." It offers an assortment of tools and templates that allow user to be artistic, thereby enhancing the appearance of word-processing documents. **Pages supports all the popular basics that can be expected from a word processor.** With the current technology, the app supports the incorporation of embedded videos, image galleries, animations, and audios.

If you are a person who likes doing different projects on your computer, Apple has good news for you. The Pages app consists of more than 70 designed templates for newsletters, resumes, flyers, books, posters, and cards. In addition to these, it is possible for you to design your own templates.

The documents in Pages are saved in a standard format for Apple, called '.pages.' Pages is also able to open and edit other common word-processing documents, including Microsoft Word. It is also possible to export your work to other formats such as rich text, plain text, PDF, and Word *(appleinsider.com, 2022)*.

Numbers

With Numbers, it is possible to add Apple visuals to spreadsheets.
The Numbers app allows you to arrange the space in a manner that is appropriate to you. Available in the Numbers app is a number of previously prepared templates, ranging from basic, business, education, and financial ones.

Hundreds of functions, be it simple or complex, are available for math-related spreadsheets. For your visual representation of data, there are bars, interactive graphs, and donut charts. **The standard format for saving documents in Numbers is '.numbers.'** It is possible to export your work to formats such as Excel and legacy *(numbers '09)*.

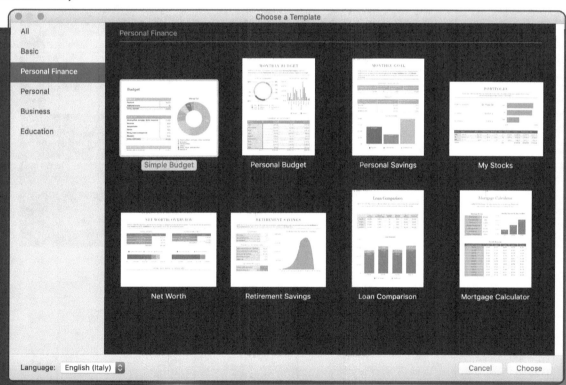

Keynote

Keynote is Apple's presentation app. Included in Keynote are customizable transitions, a number of slides, and templates made by Apple.

With Keynote, you can easily alter themes to suit your needs, embed an

audio or video, and add new slides.
Furthermore, you can alter the look of your presentation mode. **The standard format for saving Keynote documents is '.keynote.'** You can export your work to PDF, GIF, PowerPoint, and other image formats.

CHAPTER 10:

TROUBLESHOOTING, TIPS, AND TRICKS

You might face some hick-ups as you use your MacBook. With that in mind, this chapter has been created to provide you with tips and tricks that enable you to troubleshoot any challenges that you may face as you operate your Mac. You will also get insights on how to use functionalities so that you can benefit more from owning your Mac gadget. With the ideas that are provided in this chapter at your fingertips, you are set to enjoy your MacBook.

Reclaim Space

Take some time to go through your computer and search for content that you can manually delete. See if you have files, apps, or items that are no longer relevant so that you can trash them. You can also look for duplicate files that take your space unnecessarily. For instance, you might be one of those people who tend to take multiple photos that look alike. Removing some of the photos and keeping one or two representatives of each set of similar photos might leave you with extra space on your MacBook.

Deleting files or apps is pretty easy. **Simply right-click the name of the file** or the icon of the app that you want to eliminate. **Click Move to Bin and you are done.**

Please note that trashing your files and apps like this will not free space on your Mac. It's like just moving the files and apps from one part of the computer to another.

To successfully create more space on your gadget, **you also need to go into the trash and further delete the items completely.**

Make a right-click on the trash icon, prior **to clicking Empty Trash.** This action will add some kilobytes, megabytes, or gigabytes to your computer's free space.

Create ZIP Files

If you have large files that take up much space but you don't want to delete them, creating ZIP files is a viable option. ZIP files make it possible for you to compress your files so that they will take less space than they would if they had remained individual.

To create a ZIP file on your MacBook, follow these steps:

- **Identify the files that you want to ZIP.** If these files are in a folder, open it first.

- **Hold down the Command or Shift keys while you click on the files that you** intend to add to your ZIP file. These files will appear highlighted.

- **Make a right-click on the highlighted files.** Alternatively, you can click File on the menu bar that is positioned at the top of the screen.

- **Either way, click Compress X Items,** where X denotes the number of files that you highlighted with the intention to add to a ZIP file.

macbook_air.jpg

166_Pages

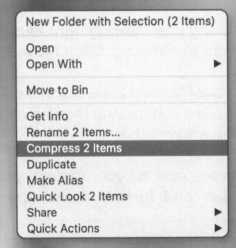

New Folder with Selection (2 Items)

Open
Open With ▶

Move to Bin

Get Info
Rename 2 Items...
Compress 2 Items
Duplicate
Make Alias
Quick Look 2 Items
Share ▶
Quick Actions ▶

ZIP

Archive.zip

Upon completing the compression, the new file will be named Archive.zip. This file will be located in the same folder where you took the compressed items from.

It's possible to change the name of the compressed file for easier identification. Prior to selecting Open, you can access the files in the ZIP folder any time by just right-clicking on it.

Unpack Your Downloads Folder

Quite often, the downloads folder ends up filled with files that were once important but not anymore. Mind you, some files even get downloaded without your consent.

If you go through this folder, you might be surprised to see videos, restaurant menus, memos, and work presentations that are no longer necessary. Clear your downloads folder often to create more free space on your computer.

To remove unwanted files in the downloads folder, start by clicking the Go Tab in Finder. To open the downloads folder, **click Downloads**. **Make right clicks** on each of the folders that you want to remove, prior to **clicking Move to Bin.**

One more tip make accessing the Downloads folder easy by creating a shortcut to it in your Dock. You can do this by dragging the Downloads folder from Finder to Dock.

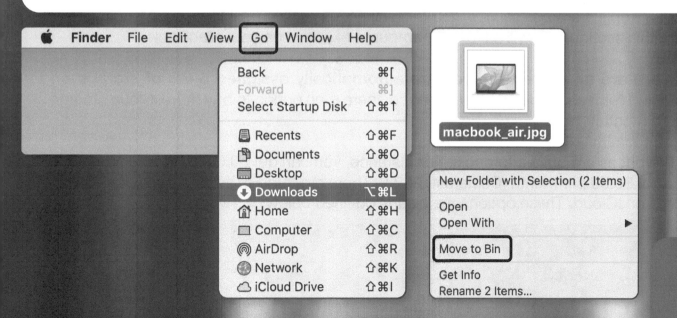

Remove Temporary Files

Temporary files accumulate as you continue to use your computer. These files occupy some of the space on the hard drive of your Mac, and more importantly, you don't need them. Therefore, clearing them off your computer can free up a lot of space. Be sure to do this often to keep them off, considering that they continue to build up as you use your Mac.

Now, how do you remove temporary files? First, **go to Finder** and **click on the tab Go**. Second, **click on Go to Folder** and then type in **~/Library/Caches. Click Go again.** After this last action, you will find yourself in a caches folder. Hightlight the files that you intend to delete and then make a right-click on them. **Select Move to Trash.** Be sure to then remove these files from your Mac's trash bin as well.

If you do not want to remove the temporary files manually, you can use the app called CleanMyMac. When you engage this app, it will not only locate the temporary files for you but also delete them.

CleanMyMac app

Use the Storage Functionality of iCloud

Instead of storing your files directly on your Mac, you can load them to iCloud. With Apple's storage service, you can still access your files with ease. More importantly for this section, you will save huge amounts of space on your MacBook.

If you are an Apple user, you are automatically assigned 5 GB of storage on iCloud for free. If you need more space, there is an option to buy more iCloud storage at a monthly fee.

The prices are quite affordable. For instance, you can get 50 GB of iCloud storage at a fee of $0.99 per month (Demarest, 2023). There are three possible options for storing files on iCloud. These options are clearly outlined below:

•   **Documents and Desktop:** All files that can occupy these folders can be stored on iCloud. In cases where the storage capacity on your Mac is low, all the other files are stored on iCloud, except for the ones that would have been recently opened. To identify the files that are stored on iCloud, check for a cloud that has an arrow pointing downwards, which is the icon for iCloud. When you want to access files that are stored in iCloud, simply click on the icon and download them.

•   **Messages:** Messages and attachments are also stored well on iCloud. You will only find the recently opened attachments and messages in your Mac, especially when the computer is low on storage.

•   **Photos:** Photos and videos are stored in their original form with full resolution. In the event that you have little space on your Mac, only the version of videos and photos that save space can be found on your computer. However, you can still get the original versions on iCloud by clicking the icon and downloading.

To store the files on your MacBook on iCloud, go to the top-left corner of your screen and **click on the Apple icon** that is located there.

Go on to select About this Mac. Click the following in their sequence: **Storage tab, Manage, and then Store in iCloud.** A pop-up menu will appear with the options of the types of files that you can store on iCloud as we described earlier. Select the ones that you want and then click Store in iCloud.

Take Out Language Files

Some of the apps that are found on your Mac come with language files associated with them. This functionality is available to accommodate different languages. However, it is more likely that you will use one language among the many that are available.

Deleting the language files that you don't use or need will actually free-up some space on your laptop. **Apps like Monolingual and CleanMyMac can delete unwanted language files for you.** With Monolingual and CleanMyMac can delete unwanted that would have been taken up by macOS language resources *(Monolingual, n.d.)*.

Back-Up Your Files

Backing up your files is one of the tricks that you will certainly need if you don't want to lose your data. You cannot overlook mishaps that affect your computer, it can even die on you. If anything should happen to your computer, you should remain at peace because your data is safe. In this section, we will look at different ways through which you can keep your data safe and accessible.

TAKE ADVANTAGE OF THE TIME MACHINE

Time Machine

The Time Machine is Apple's own back-up software that is part of the macOS. To use the Time Machine for backing up your files, plug in an external storage device: USB, SSD, or hard drive. A NAS drive that will connect to your Mac through a WI-FI network will also work.

Here is the procedure that you can follow for you to set up Time Machine on your Mac:

1. **Ensure that external storage is connected to your MacBook.**

2. **The external storage should be formatted as Mac OS Extended (Journaled).** If the formatting is correct, be on the lookout for an alert on your Mac, inquiring

whether you would want to use the connected drive with Time Machine. Go on and click Use as a Backup Disk.

3.   In the event that the alert does not appear, **open System Preferences and go to Time Machine Preferences.** Here, **select Backup Disk** before choosing the storage device of your choice. Now, **click Use Disk.**

4.   **You can encrypt your backup if you choose to.** If you encrypt your backups, be sure to keep your password handy because it will become a requirement before you can access your files.

One thing that you will also need to remember when you use the Time Machine is to plug the external hard drive into your computer. Otherwise, no backup will be happening.

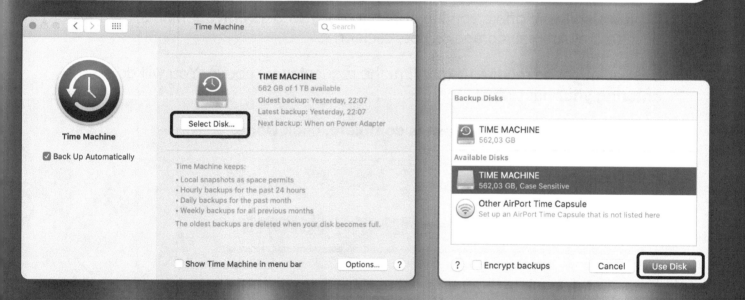

USE A BACKUP SOFTWARE THAT'LL CLONE YOUR MAC'S HARD DRIVE

These backup software will duplicate the information that is on the hard drive of your computer. Carbon Copy Cloner, Acronis, SuperDuper, and ChronoSync are good examples of such cloning software.

As is the case with the Time Machine, you need to plug in your hard drive before you can use cloning software.

The step-by-step guide on how to clone your MacBook highly depends on the type of software that you choose. However, the procedure for all the software won't deviate much from the following steps:

1. **Start by connecting your external storage to your Mac.**

2. If there is a need for you to format the drive, prior to use, open Disk Utility. **Select the external drive, click Erase, and then select macOS Extended (Journaled).** Again, click on Erase.

3. **Now, go to the cloning software and open it.**

4. If the software offers you the option to copy what is on your Mac's internal hard drive to the external storage device, click on it.

5. You might be required to confirm the request in (4) above. You will do so by **entering your password.**

6. **Once the copying process is complete, click Done.**

Backup your Files using iCloud

You can safely back up your files using iCloud. If you pay a monthly subscription for iCloud storage, you can access more space so you can backup more files. Without a subscription, you are limited to the 5 GB that you get by virtue of being a user of Apple.

Backing up your information on iCloud is a great idea, especially when you have more than one MacBook. This strategy may also come in handy when you want to access your information from, say, an iPhone.

Google Drive or Dropbox

Dropbox Google Drive

If for any reason you can't use iCloud for backing up your files, Google Drive and Dropbox are viable alternatives. Although these strategies are usually used for sharing files, especially during collaborations, you can also opt for them as backup methods. However, Dropbox and Google Drive are more appropriate for backing smaller or fewer files than the ones that iCloud can hold. You can access the files that you backup through Dropbox from any other computer.

Here is how you can use Dropbox as a backup option:

1. **Sign up for a Dropbox account**, before you download and install the application's software.

2. **Open Dropbox on your Mac**.

3. On the right, **click on Upload Folder or Upload Files**. Identify the folder that you would like to upload and then click Choose. Give your Mac some time to complete the upload.

4. It's also possible to drag the folders or files from their location on your Mac to Dropbox through Finder.

Recover Files From Backup

Having transferred your files to a backup drive or software, how then would you get them back to your Mac if need be? This question will be answered in this section. Let's go!

USING MIGRATION ASSISTANT
If you used the Time Machine for backup, the migration assistant is the right tool to use when you want to recover your files.

Using this tool might need you to reinstall your macOS, which you should do before you can continue. To begin, your Time Machine should be connected to your Mac.

Also, **ensure that the Time Machine disk is switched on**. Now, **go to your Mac and open Migration Assistant. You will find it in the Utilities folder, inside the Applications folder.**

You will be asked about how you prefer to transfer the files.Go for the option to transfer from a Mac, startup disk, or Time Machine backup prior to clicking Continue. Click Time Machine backup and then Continue. Select a backup and then click Continue again. Identify the information that you want to transfer and select it.

To begin the transfer, click Continue. Please note that the length of the time that it takes for your transfer to compete varies with the size of the files.

Run First Aid From macOS Utilities

Are you facing regular app and/or system crashes? Could it be that some of your files are becoming corrupted, while some simply vanish?

When you start facing these issues on your Mac, running first aid from macOS utilities might just save the day. This intervention also works when your Mac is taking far too long to start up, apart from other start-up problems.

If external devices are not working as expected or you keep getting cryptic error messages, then running the first aid is the way to go. This section will enlighten you on what you need to do to run first aid from macOS Utilities.

Once you diagnose the problems that we mentioned earlier in this section, the first step that you should take is to backup all your data, if you weren't doing so already. After that, you can go on and deal with the Disk Utility.

It is normal to feel a bit skeptical about touching this area but there is no need for you to fear because it's quite an easy procedure. Follow these steps:

1. **To open the Disk Utility, go to Finder. Click Applications and then select Utilities.**

2. In the sidebar, identify the disk that is giving you challenges and select it.

3. Right at the top, **click on First Aid** ⟨ 🩺 ⟩ **and then Run.**

4. Upon completion, check for a dropdown menu that shows the status of the disk. When you click on it, you will get more information about the issue at hand.

Apparently, Disk Utility will make efforts to repair as much damage as possible. It will let you know of the available errors that it cannot correct.

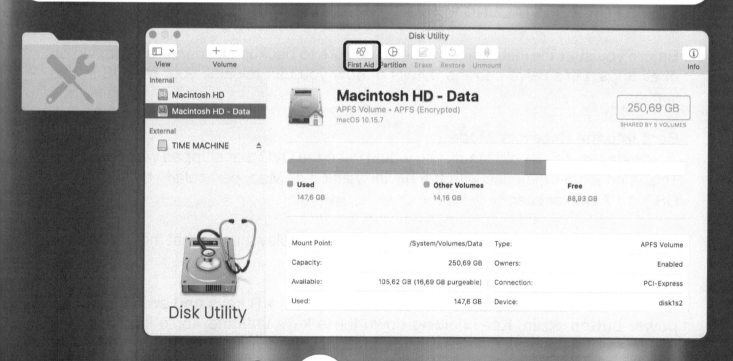

Reinstall macOS to Solve Severe Problems

Reinstalling macOS usually sounds like an extreme intervention to problems on your Mac. However, there are severe problems that may require drastic measures for them to be solved. In this section, we will look at how you can successfully reinstall macOS on your MacBook. However, before we do that, we will explore some of the problems that might require you to reinstall macOS.

You might need to reinstall macOS when

- **Your machine becomes super slow in operating.**
- **You keep getting error messages.**
- **Your MacBook refuses to boot.**
- **Softwares fail to run correctly.**

STEPS FOR REINSTALLING MACOS

Before you start the installation process, be sure to backup all your files. Also, log out of all apps. Let's delve into the details of how you can reinstall your macOS in this section.

Boot Into the Recovery Mode

To reinstall the OS for old Macs, you would need the DVD that shipped with your Mac. This is no longer the case with the newer version of Mac, particularly those running OS X 10.7 Lion or later.

For the modern Macs, the built-in recovery mode will play the role that the DVD played in old Macs.

To boot your Mac, shut it down first. Hold the Cmd + R keys and switch on the power button again. Keep holding down these keys until the Apple logo appears. Within a few seconds, a macOS Utilities page that has a variety of options will appear.

In some instances, your computer might fail to pass the Apple logo stage by freezing. If this happens, opt for the internet recovery mode. Taking this step means that the recovery environment will now be run from the internet, not your hard drive.

To start the internet Recovery mode, press Cmd + Option + R. This time expect a spinning globe, not the Apple logo.

After the startup process, make sure you are connected to a Wi-Fi network. Give your Mac enough time to download the recovery environment. Select your language. Please note that the system may reinstall a version of macOS that is different from the one that you had before you used the Internet Recovery mode. For instance, you might get Lion, when you initially had Mavericks.

Erase the Disk

Please note that you can skip this step if you don't want to lose any data upon reinstalling your macOS. However, if you want to follow all the steps, then you have to erase the disk. To start this process, **go to the menu and click Disk Utility**. After this, check the options on the left sidebar and **choose your internal hard drive.**

This drive is usually labeled as Macintosh HD. On the right side, there is an Erase tab; click it. **Check to see that the format appears as Mac OS Extended (Journaled).** By **clicking Erase,** you will be confirming the operation. After this procedure, it's time to reinstall your macOS so quit the Disk Utility by holding down the Cmd + Q keys.

Reinstall macOS

Now that you have completed clearing your information off your computer, you can reinstall your macOS. Doing this depends on how you booted your computer.

Suppose you booted it from a USB disk, then you should click Continue and you will be taken to the installer. In the event that you booted it from a functioning recovery partition, go to the **Restore macOS button and click it.** This will trigger the installation process to begin. When you get to a point where you are asked which hard drive you would want to install your macOS onto, select the Macintosh HD because it is the one that you selected earlier on.

Please take note that the installation of macOS might take some time, so be patient and do not disturb it. Soon after the installation is complete, your Mac will restart on its own and you will be requested to create an account. Follow the prompts and enjoy improved functionalities on your Mac!

The Genius Bar to Resolve Troubleshoot

The Genius Bar is the support counter that is found at Apple store locations. The employees who work there are well trained at the corporate headquarters for Apple. They are experts in dealing with technical issues pertaining to software and hardware. Therefore, if you want assistance with troubleshooting issues on your device, the Genius Bar is the place to go.

Please note that the Genius Bar does not fix problems that are associated with your cellular service. Moreover, the Genius Bar does not guarantee that the problem that you are facing with your device will be resolved it all depends on the type of problem. However, in most cases, the issues are resolved.

To get services at a Genius Bar, be sure to book an appointment, and please do so ahead of time. The first step in doing this is to go to the Apple website: apple.com.

At the bottom of the screen, click the Apple Retail Store link. When the link opens, **go down to the Genius Bar section** and select Learn more about the Genius Bar. On the right side of the screen, find the Genius Bar Reservations tab and click it. You will be prompted to choose a state and location. Upon following the prompts that appear on the screen, you will book your appointment.

Be prepared to pay for the services from the Genius Bar, unless your device is still covered on a limited warranty. Please note that the warranty only works for you in this case if the issues on your device are due to bad workmanship or parts that are faulty. If the damage is due to mishandling practices or accidents like falling, you will have to pay for the services that you get at the Genius Bar.

Be sure to back up your information before you take your device to the Genius Bar because there's a chance that some of the information in your device might disappear during the troubleshooting processes, depending on the type of problem being resolved. Therefore, ensure that all your videos, music, contacts, and apps are synced through iCloud or iTunes. This way, you will have a backup copy of your valuable data.

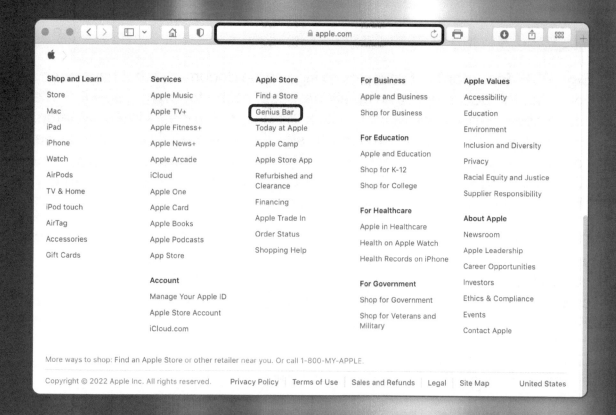

More Tips and Tricks

At this point, you might have gained a lot of knowledge about navigating through your Mac, as well as taking care of it. In this section, you will learn more tips and tricks that will lay a great foundation for you to become an expert in dealing with your Mac. Here are some of the fascinating ideas that you will be glad to have come across:

- **Swap between desktops:** If you are using multiple desktops, switching between them is quite easy. Simply press the Control button and then punch the left or right arrow.

- **Copying links:** Do you want to copy links faster in Safari? **Simultaneously press Command and L so that you highlight the URL bar.** To copy, **press Command and C.**

- **Quick access to the dictionary:** Suppose you find a word that you do not understand, highlight the word and then press on it with the Force Touch Trackpad. A dictionary definition of the highlighted word will appear on your screen.

- **Sign PDF documents:** If you want to sign some documents that have been sent to you, drag the document to an email message. At the top right, you will find a button with a down arrow. Click Markup. Click the box that appears like a signature. Click Trackpad and then use the mouse to sign on to the trackpad. Alternatively, you can write your signature on a white sheet and then capture this signature using Webcam. To do this, click Camera to show that this is the option that you are choosing. Save the signature for recurrent use.

- **Create your own keyboard shortcut:** There are default keyboard shortcuts that you might be used to. Did you know that you can create your own keyboard box with the option for you to choose the application of choice? You will also be prompted to choose the menu command and keyboard shortcut that you prefer. Finish off by clicking Add and you are all set!

- **Get invisible files in Finder:** No more troubles getting the invisible files in Finder anymore. Simply click **Cmd, Shift, and the period (.).**

- **Resizing a window:** There are many other options that you can use to resize the window but most of them shift the proportions of the window. To avoid this problem, press Shift as you simultaneously resize the window from the corner or edge. When you use this method, the window is resized from the center interesting, isn't it?

- **Extending battery life:** There are a number of available options that can assist you to extend the battery life of your Mac. These include turning off the WiFi and Bluetooth, doing away with runaway applications, ensuring Spotlight indexing is turned off, lowering the brightness of your screen, and turning-off Time Machine. You can even select Energy Saver Preferences and keep them on.

- **Creating an auto duplicating file:** If there is a file that you want to open in duplicate click the file, right-click, and then choose Get Info. Go to the Stationary Pad Box and check it. Once you do tthat, the file will opena duplicate whenver you click it This comes in handy when you are dealing with templates.

- **Hiding a window:** Hiding a window from your desktop can be quicker than you can imagine. Just press Command and H and the window will disappear. Pressing Command and Tab will bring the hidden window back

CONCLUSION

As you grow older, you might have more time for yourself and your family, considering that you might have retired as well. Your Mac might be your best acquaintance, even though your family and friends are miles away. This device might be a tool for communication with your loved ones, in addition to assisting you with access to entertainment and information. With the fast-paced advances in technology, you can use your MacBook to do various things like making payments. However, you need to know how to use the device in order for you to enjoy the benefits of owning one. This book comes in handy because it provides you with a comprehensive guide on how to use and deal with your Mac.

This book starts with enlightening you on various terms that you are more likely to come across as you use your Mac. These terms include software, hardware, app, browser, CPU, and Wi-Fi, just to mention a few. Knowing these terms helps you to understand the step-by-step guidelines that are outlined in this book. We also highlighted the different types of MacBooks, which are MacBook Air, MacBook Pro, and iMac. Please note that the MacBook Pro can be with or without a touch bar. If you have eyesight issues, the MacBook with a larger screen is a great choice, that is if you don't have one already.

Guidelines on how to start-up your Mac are clearly explained in this book, along with other ideas for customizing the Dock so that its appearance appeals to you. Some of the tasks that you want to complete on your Mac require the internet, which is why this book taught you about how to connect to Wi-Fi. Not only that but tips on choosing the right browser were also brought forward. We zeroed into the Safari browser because it is the brainchild of Apple. All this is meant to make your experience on the internet as enjoyable as it can possibly be.

If you use your Mac for entertainment purposes, you are more likely to navigate through different media such as music, videos, and pictures. Not to worry, this book explained how you can use these functionalities. You can even share media with others as described.

Here are even more tasks that you can compete with your Mac:

- **Receiving and sending emails**
- **Starting and receiving FaceTime calls**
- **Chatting through messages**
- **Taking selfies using Photo Booth**
- **Reading books**
- **Watching TV and movies**
- **Exploring the world using Maps**

If you are staying with children who might also need to access your Mac, you can create accounts for them that are separate from yours. Doing this allows you to plan and monitor the type of activities that the children can become exposed to. This protects the minors from information that is possibly toxic to them. There are various other security features that are available on your Mac. You can access these System Preferences, which is the pane where you can customize the settings of your computer to match your needs and wants.

In the event that you have problems with your Mac, this book provided you with tips for troubleshooting them. For example, if your Wi-Fi does seem to work, restarting your Mac might just solve the issue. If your gadget is becoming slower when completing tasks, it might be low on space. Ideas and tips for reclaiming your space—deleting some files and apps, creating ZIP files, and getting rid of temporary files - were highlighted as well.

In the case that you have been unable to solve the problems that are affecting the proper functioning of your computer, you can book an appointment with the Genius Bar that is nearest to you. At the Genius Bar, your gadget will be checked by experts who have been properly trained to do so.

Please note that it is crucial for you to backup your information when you take your Mac to the Genius Bar. There are several backup strategies that you can use. You can use Time Machine, iCloud, and Dropbox as backup tools. Serious problems on your Mac might prompt you to reinstall your macOS. Again, this measure requires that you backup your data.

The book ends by giving you some tips that make your navigation through your Mac as easy and fast as possible. For instance, you can create your own keyboard shortcuts, in addition to the ones that default to your Mac like the Command plus C for copying. Did you know that just pressing the Control button while punching the left or right arrow is another way for switching between desktops? It's even much easier than the conventional way of switching from one desktop to the other. It is my hope that as you get to the end of this book, you will have gained a lot of insights and confidence to navigate through your Mac.

Happy MacBook Exploring!

MacBook Air

FREE BONUS

**To Download your FREE BONUS
Turn On Your Cellphone Camera,
Focus it on the Code Below
and Click the Link that Appears**

OR

**Go to:
https://rb.gy/zmzvfl**

Made in United States
Troutdale, OR
12/21/2023

16269931R00097